# BRITAIN

## Susan Cohen

SHIRE LIVING HISTORIES

How we worked • How we pla we lived

D1494921

SHIRE PUBLICATIONS
Bloomsbury Publishing Plc

PO Box 883, Oxford, OX1 9PL, UK
1385 Broadway, 5th Floor, New York, NY 10018, USA
Email: shire@bloomsbury.com

SHIRE is a trademark of Osprey Publishing, a division of
Bloomsbury Publishing Plc

© 2014 Shire Publications

First published in Great Britain in 2014 by Shire Publications

Transferred to digital print-on-demand in 2019

Printed and bound in Great Britain.

A CIP catalogue record for this book is available from the British
Library.

Shire Living History no. 15. ISBN-13: 978 0 74781 285 2

PDF ebook ISBN: 978 1 78442 006 2

ePub ebook ISBN: 978 1 78442 005 5

Susan Cohen has asserted her right under the Copyright, Designs and
Patents Act, 1988, to be identified as the author of this book.

Designed by Tony Truscott Designs, UK and typeset in Janson Text,
Perpetua and Gill Sans.

**www.shirebooks.co.uk**
To find out more about our authors and books visit our website. Here
you will find extracts, author interviews, details of forthcoming events
and the option to sign-up for our newsletter.

COVER IMAGE
A street in the north of the UK, c. 1964. (Getty images/Halton
Archive)

TITLE PAGE IMAGE
Children playing on a bomb-site in Manchester, 1960s.

CONTENTS PAGE IMAGE
Members of the 59 Club outside St Martin in the Fields
church, London, to support Christian Aid, 24 May 1964. The
59 Club started in 1959 as a Church of England-based youth
club in Hackney Wick, London. It was adopted by 'rockers' in
the early 1960s. Father Graham Hullett was one of the eight
founder members and in 1967 became the club's first full-time
youth worker.

ACKNOWLEDGEMENTS
Mike Ashworth, David Bagnall, Matthew Bradby, Duncan Chew,
Roger Curd, Emil Dudek, Roger Billington, Carol Bolton, Kevin
Danks, Stephen Dowle, Geoff Dowling, Stephen Dunderdale, Lauren
England, Tony Hall, Saffron Herbert, Robert Higgins, Morton
Hill, Gavin Hill-Smith/The AA, Simon Hingley, Colette Hobbs,
Tony Houston, Philip Howard, Michael Hughes, Keith Lovell, Paul
Kennelly, Mike Leale, Mark Lennon, Luke Massey, Sarah de Mellow,
Brian Middleton, Stephen Musgrave, Mark Norton, Colin O'Brien,
Chris Oldham, James Poyner, Phil Rix, Paul Seaton, Gemma Shaw,
Homer Sykes, Peter Trulock.

PHOTOGRAPH ACKNOWLEDGEMENTS
Advertising Archives, page 21; Alamy, page 72; Mike Ashworth
Collection, pages 24, 65 (right); The Automobile Association, page
66; David Bagnall, page 14–15; BT.com Archives, page 83; Butlin's
Archive, page 34; Butlin's Memories, page 25; Mick Taylor/Campaign
for Nuclear Disarmament Archives, page 9; Cheshire Constabulary,
page 13 (top); Cowley Local History Society, page 86; Roger Curd,
page 65 (left); Kevin Danks/R. A. Gibson, pages 30, 58, 62; Stephen
Dowle, page 64; Geoff Dowling, page 41 (bottom); The Downs School,
West Berkshire, page 55; Emil Dudek/ www.vintage-technology.
info/, page 71; Stephen Dunderdale, page 70; Dusashenka, page
78; Ercol, page 47 (bottom); Grace's Guide, pages 47 (top), 49, 89;
Greater Manchester Police Museum and Archives, page 63; Robert
Higgins, page 48; Simon Hingley/ www.riverdale.co.uk, page 54;
Tony Houston, page 12; Philip Howard, pages 16, 20; HSBC archives,
page 80; Michael Hughes, page 74; IPC Media Syndication, pages 21
(bottom), 60; Diane Langleben, page 76; Mike Leale, page 31; Lenton
Sands, page 17; Longmeadow Infants (now Primary) School, Herts.,
page 52; Midlands Co-operative Society, page 40; Brian Middleton,
page 22; Mirrorpix, pages 3, 4, 8, 10, 13 (bottom), 32, 38, 44, 68,
79, 84, 88, 91; Stephen Musgrave, page 57; Dennis J. Norton, page
67 (bottom); Colin O'Brien, pages 6, 18–19, 42, 46; James Poyner,
pages 1, 59; Barnet Saidman/The Queen's Nursing Institute, page
93; Rex Features, page 77; Phil Rix/www.airliners.net, pages 26–7;
Paul Seaton/Woolworths Virtual Museum, pages 50, 51, 73, 82; Pete
Spooner, page 33; PizzaExpress.com, page 35; South West Image Bank,
pages 11, 41 (top); Homer Sykes, page 85; Peter Trulock, page 67
(top); Michael West, page 75; West Wales Museum of Childhood, page
23; Victoria and Albert Museum Collection, page 36.

# CONTENTS

# PREFACE

M ANY PEOPLE have been credited with saying, 'if you can remember the sixties, you weren't there'. Whoever it was, they were wrong. There was far more to the 1960s than the Beatles or psychedelic shirts on the King's Road. It was a decade in which the welfare state began to realise its original promise, starting to offer genuine improvements in the lives of many people, and before its inherent contradictions and unfeasible cost began to loom as large as they later would. With the grim reality of working-class life repeated and unflinchingly portrayed on the screen and stage, the resultant determination to forge a better life for all citizens was palpable.

It was a time of buoyant modernism and genuine optimism, right across society, with a mood of liberal rebellion against the shackles of Victorian values, and uncritical enthusiasm for the United States politically, and for American popular culture more generally.

Susan Cohen's look at British life in the years 1960–69 provides a balanced correction to the many studies of the period that focus on the music, the media and the sensational lifestyles of the most privileged. She finds the 1960s as much in the grimy reality of lower-middle-class high streets and the football pools, as in the *Lady Chatterley* trial or *The Avengers*. Despite this she is happy to acknowledge the many and real changes for the better that occurred: the prosperity that meant that wartime rationing – which had continued to the mid-1950s – soon seemed unimaginable; and the wholesale demolition of Victorian slums and their replacement with estates and high-rise blocks designed (not entirely successfully) to achieve a new and better environment for their inhabitants.

With its fascinating mixture of reportage photographs, popular culture imagery and forgotten details of life, this book allows all those whose drug-fuelled lifestyle meant that they have forgotten the 1960s to find out what they missed.

Peter Furtado
General Editor

Opposite:
The death of Sir Winston Churchill sent waves of emotion throughout the land, and more than 320,000 people filed past his body as it lay in state at Westminster Cathedral before his state funeral on 30 January 1965.

# INTRODUCTION

THE POPULAR IMAGE of 1960s Britain is of the 'Swinging Sixties', a golden age in which the whole nation was enjoying a wonderful party. The decade was certainly characterised by enormous social, economic, cultural and political change, much of it accompanied or even driven by a new optimism. This confidence was underpinned by finance, with people able to move up the economic ladder, and the big picture was one of full employment. But there was also a ruthless process of self-ridicule, which emerged in the form of satire that challenged this same optimism. Besides this there was genuine public concern over the 'brain drain', the exodus of British talent, especially in the scientific, academic and technical arenas, mostly to the USA, which was fuelled by high taxation and lack of opportunity. State censorship came to an end and a climate prevailed in which entrepreneurs and innovators were able to thrive, driven by consumer demand, creating everything from consumer opportunities to medical advances. At the start of the decade society at large was patriotic, class conscious and cautious, accepting of gender and race inequalities and accustomed to the traditional role of men as breadwinners and women as homemakers. National Service was coming to an end with the last call-ups made in December 1960. Divorce and illegitimacy were stigmatised, homosexuality and abortion were illegal, and the punishment for murder was the death penalty. The baby-boom generation, born in the mid- to late 1940s, were the new teenagers of the 1960s – more than five million at the start of the decade – and their outlook, values and expectations were very different from those of their parents; these both shaped them and their environment. They enjoyed enhanced educational, employment and cultural opportunities, unheard-of freedom and spending power. But the relentless pace of change was uneven, for by contrast there were millions of people, especially in the north-east and west, the industrial heartlands, south Wales and central Scotland, as well as the poorer areas of London and other big cities, whose lives changed very little. They continued to suffer from

Opposite:
A back street in
Bolton in the early
1960s.

7

unemployment, homelessness, isolation and poverty, and immigrants, many of whom were economic migrants, were subjected to prejudice and racism.

Economically, the decade began inauspiciously. The Conservative government's 1959 tax-cutting measures were proving ineffective, and when prime minister Harold Macmillan appointed Selwyn Lloyd as chancellor of the exchequer in July 1960, the trade gap was widening and industrial unrest was crippling the docks, the car and the construction industries. The pattern continued in early 1961, with walk outs and rejected pay demands leading to staff 'working to rule'. Selwyn Lloyd's deflationary 'Little Budget', and legally unenforceable pay freeze on the public sector, failed to squeeze domestic demand and reduce imports. As austerity bit, so public support for Macmillan diminished, only to be compounded by the loss of the Orpington by-election to the Liberals in March 1962. Worse followed on 13 July, the 'Night of the Long Knives', when details of Macmillan's dramatic Cabinet reshuffle, which ousted Selwyn Lloyd and five other Cabinet ministers, was leaked in advance to the press. There were,

Labour Party general election campaign, 6 October 1964, with Harold Wilson addressing a rally at Wandsworth Town Hall.

DOUGLAS JAY
BATTERSEA NORTH

JAY

Dr DAVID KERR
WANDSWORTH CENTRAL

Let's
GO
with
LABOUR

ERNEST PERRY
BATTERSEA SOUTH

VOTE
PERRY

CND: Over the Easter weekend of 1962, thousands of protesters marched from the atomic weapons establishment at Aldermaston, Berkshire to Trafalgar Square, London, under the banner of the Campaign for Nuclear Disarmament. The pilgrimage became an annual event.

meanwhile, the on-going pressures of the Cold War: 22 October 1962 was indelibly etched in people's minds as the first day of the Cuban missile crisis, when the world was brought to the edge of a nuclear war. Added to this was the sentencing to eighteen years' imprisonment of John Vassall, a former cipher clerk in the British Embassy in Moscow, then a civil servant in the Admiralty, who pleaded guilty to spying for the Soviet Union, and in 1963 the defection of Kim Philby, formerly head of the Soviet section of MI5, and unmasked as a KGB mole. The last straw for the ailing Macmillan was the Profumo affair, caused by the secretary of state for war's sexual liaison with a call girl, Christine Keeler. Profumo resigned on 5 June 1963, having caused irreparable damage to the party, and Macmillan, who had also failed in his efforts to get Britain into the European Common Market, followed suit in October. A month later, on 22 November, the President of the United States, John Kennedy, was assassinated in Dallas, Texas, an event that echoed across the world. At home, and to the surprise of many in Parliament, the aristocratic Alec Douglas-Home was appointed new prime minister, but his tenure was short lived, for when the country went to the polls in October 1964, Harold Wilson won with a narrow majority of five seats, on the back of his promise to modernise the country.

January 1965 was tinged with sadness as the nation mourned the death of Sir Winston Churchill, but was jolted back to reality with

Aberfan, 21 October 1966. For a moment, the digging stops as another body is brought out from the shattered school. The tribunal inquiry that followed the disaster laid the blame squarely on the National Coal Board, but no member was ever prosecuted, sacked or even reprimanded.

the launch of Labour's National Plan for economic development. Hanging for murder was suspended for an experimental five years and Wilson laid the foundations for a 'University in the Air', which later became the Open University. Immigration was once again on the political agenda, precipitated by the arrival of thousands of Kenyan Asians fleeing Africa, providing a target for the British National Party, formed in 1960 by the merger of the National Labour Party and the White Defence League. The 1962 Commonwealth Immigrants Act was tightened again in 1965, further restricting entry, while the Race Relations Act banned discrimination in public places and criminalised incitement to racial hatred. The Race Relations Board was set up the following year.

Labour's position was greatly strengthened after the general election on 31 March 1966, when they were returned to power with a majority of ninety-eight, but the economy was in a dire state and the National Plan was seriously challenged. In an attempt at curbing

raging inflation, Harold Wilson – who in opposition had been the champion of the low paid and the trade unions – announced a six-month wage and price freeze on 'Black Wednesday', 20 July. Fortunately for him, the nation's morale was boosted ten days later by England's football team winning the world cup.

Several crimes in the 1960s gave the perpetrators undeserved publicity. Despite causing a death, the audacity of the fifteen-member gang of Great Train Robbers in August 1963, led by Ronnie Biggs, provided them with an unwarranted measure of celebrity status. The heinous crimes of the Moors murderers, Myra Hindley and Ian Brady, who came to trial in 1966, raised concerns of a possible link between moral permissiveness, evident in the relaxation of censorship, and an increase in violent offences against the person, with figures rising from 11,592 in 1960 to 15,976 in 1964. The tragedy of Aberfan, south Wales on 21 October 1966 – when the Merthyr Vale Colliery tip crashed down the mountainside, engulfed Pantglas Junior School and demolished eleven cottages killing 144 people, including 116 children with five of their teachers – had a sobering effect across the country. Environmental concerns were raised in March 1967, when the tanker, *Torrey Canyon*, ran aground off Land's End, Cornwall, and leaked crude oil. Some 15,000 sea birds were killed and British experts later calculated that the chemical detergents used in the cleaning-up process were responsible for 90 per cent of the damage to plant and animal life. This was also the year that homosexuality ceased to be a crime, with the passing of the Sexual Offences Act. Misery mounted at home as an oil embargo began on 6 June 1967. This was the outcome of a joint Arab decision to deter countries, including Britain, from supporting Israel, following the outbreak of the Six-Day War the previous day. The effect on the economy was compounded by dock strikes that spread from Liverpool to London, by an outbreak of foot and mouth disease, and by a disastrous train

On 28 May 1967, Francis Chichester sailed into Plymouth, having single-handedly circumnavigated the world in his yacht, *Gipsy Moth IV*.

Anti-Vietnam protesters in Regent Street, London, 17 March 1968. The protesters moved on from Trafalgar Square to the American Embassy in Grosvenor Square, where mounted police with batons charged at them.

Opposite top: This dairy farm in Cheshire was one of many badly affected by the foot-and-mouth outbreak. The disease was first discovered at Bryn Farm, Shropshire in October 1967, and despite quarantines and the banning of general animal movement, the virus rapidly spread, and over the course of six months, 430,000 animals across 2,300 British farms were slaughtered.

derailment at Hither Green, south London on 5 November, when forty-nine people were killed.

The new year of 1968 burst into life with the short-lived and largely unsuccessful 'I'm Backing Britain' campaign, inspired by five typists from Surbiton, Surrey, who, against all union principles, decided to work an extra half an hour every day unpaid. The year was soon defined by the number of protests, much of them aimed at the Wilson government whose promises of progressive politics had not materialised. Peace in Vietnam was at the heart of the student demonstrations in London, the first on 17 March where 25,000 people congregated in Trafalgar Square. In the midst of these protests, the findings of a Political and Economic Planning Ltd. survey, published in 1967, confirmed rising racial discrimination, and the spectre of racial hatred loomed as more Kenyan Asian refugees arrived in the country – around 23,000 between 1965 and 1967. As a consequence, home secretary James Callaghan rushed the Commonwealth Immigrants Bill through Parliament in February 1968 which tightened up entry and was voted against by all the Liberal MPs along with thirty-five Labour members and fifteen Conservatives. This was swiftly followed by a reinforced Race Relations Bill, which prohibited discrimination in housing, employment and commercial services. The most vociferous opponent to incomers was the Conservative MP Enoch Powell whose racist predictions, articulated in his speech in Birmingham on 20 April 1968, were greeted with enthusiastic applause by his audience. Elsewhere his remarks were considered extraordinarily inflammatory and resulted in him being sacked by Edward Heath. The Race Relations Act came into force in November 1968, paving the way for a more just multi-ethnic British society.

March 1969 saw the infamous Kray twins finally sentenced to life imprisonment, while in Northern Ireland, a 105-day siege, known as 'The Battle of the Bogside', began, and the first contingent of 300 British troops was deployed on a temporary basis. Operation *Banner* would in fact last thirty-eight years. Months later Neil Armstrong became the first man to walk on the moon on 21 July 1969, and his words, 'That's one small step for man, one giant leap for mankind' became indelibly etched in people's minds. Months later, on 1 October, the Anglo-French airliner Concorde completed its first supersonic flight, travelling at roughly 1,400 mph, twice the speed of sound. As the decade closed the annual violent crimes figure exceeded 21,000 and on 16 December 1969 MPs voted by a big majority for the permanent abolition of the death penalty for murder.

Below left: This Stanley Franklin cartoon, with its reference to Enoch Powell's racist attitudes, appeared in the *Daily Mirror* on 13 November 1969.

Following page: Members of the royal family leaving Wales after the investiture of twenty-year-old Prince Charles as the twenty-first Prince of Wales. Four thousand guests witnessed him receiving the insignia from the Queen during the ceremony at Caernarfon Castle on 1 July 1969. Left to right, the Queen Mother, Princess Alice, Princess Margaret, Prince Philip and the Queen.

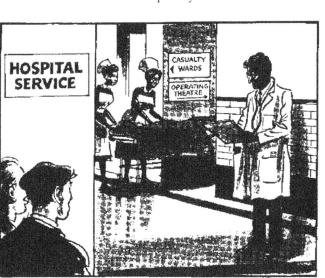

"Is this some of the 'Alien-occupied territory' Powell's talking about?"

# FAMILY

Nᴇᴡ ᴏᴘᴘᴏʀᴛᴜɴɪᴛɪᴇs, high levels of employment and a feeling of confidence in the economy were reflected in generally increased standards of living and greater longevity. By the end of the 1960s women could expect to live to seventy-four, men to sixty-nine. There were around 16 million households in 1961, 18 per cent of which comprised an adult couple and one or two children, while around 8 per cent were families of a couple and three or more children. As neighbourhoods were dismantled

The institution of marriage reached unprecedented levels of popularity in the 1960s, and the numbers of weddings rose from around 340,000 in 1961 to a peak in 1969 of around 390,000. Ninety-five per cent of men and 96 per cent of women under the age of forty-five were married. Taken by E. Parkin of Trowel.

generations of families who had lived in close proximity were split up. Young brides were still the norm, and David Williams recalled that when his twin brothers married during the 1960s, their brides were only sixteen and seventeen. For all the talk of promiscuity, a survey undertaken for the *Sunday Times* late in the decade found that pre-marital sex was less common than popularly thought. A quarter of the men and nearly two-thirds of the women questioned said they were virgins when they married, and the fear of an unwanted pregnancy was ever present. The oral contraceptive, or the 'pill', was first marketed in Britain in 1963, but was neither free nor available to unmarried women. The Family Planning Association did not officially begin providing contraceptive advice to single women until 1966, and even though the Family Planning Act (1967) allowed local authorities to provide free family planning services, only about one quarter did so, so the benefits were slow and uneven throughout the decade.

These were the so-called baby-boom years, with the birth rate in the UK reaching an all-time high in 1964, 30 per cent above the 1955 level. But in 1964, around 7.2 per cent of live births – 63,000 – were illegitimate, and family and public disapproval, the lack of adequate social and financial support was, as Baroness Summerskill pointed out, 'a tragic problem to the unmarried mother.' Most had to give up their infant, resulting in some 40,000 adoptions. Girls were frequently separated from their babies at the mother-and-baby home where they had been sent, or straight from hospital, like one young woman whose parents drove her from Manchester to a convent in Liverpool where she handed over her ten-day-old baby to a nun – the baby was never mentioned again. Some 80,000

Opposite:
Boys scrubbing the dormitory floor at the National Children's Home, 1960s. The sooner they finished the sooner they could go out to play. They wore wellington boots, or, in this instance, went barefoot, so they did not have to clean and polish their leather shoes or sandals afterwards.

CLOSED
FROM £30 OR
ON EASY TERMS
MORPHY-RICHARDS
Electrolux
Prestcold

Baby transport changed in the 1960s as old-fashioned carriage-built prams like this one, unsuitable for flat dwellers and cars, were replaced by light carry cots that fitted onto a folding wheeled frame. The Maclaren buggy, patented in 1965, revolutionised pushchairs, and appealed to fathers, who otherwise did little towards childcare.

children in Britain were in foster care, which was hugely expensive, costing around £9 a week in an institution compared with 'boarding out' at between £2 and £4 a week. Most children in London care homes, where the pressure was greatest, could expect to be there until they were fifteen or sixteen.

Despite the popularity of marriage, an increasing number of couples sought divorce. There were an average of 37,657 divorce

Even the smallest children, including these five-year-old girls, were given simple chores at the National Children's Home in the 1960s.

petitions each year between 1961 and 1965, and of the 57,089 annually between 1966 and 1969, around 63 per cent were initiated by women. The impact of the liberalising Divorce Reform Act of 1969, which allowed divorce after two years of separation by mutual agreement, was yet to be felt. However, the stigma of divorce lingered, as Wendy Mitchell remembered: for eight years, from the age of eight, she kept her parents' divorce a secret from even her best friends at school.

According to the 1961 census, 26 per cent of all mothers of dependent children worked, and

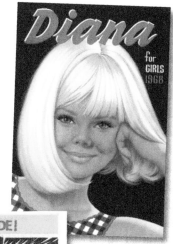

Adventure comics for boys included *Smash* which ran for 257 issues, between February 1966 and April 1971, and *Valiant* (1962–71). Popular girls comics included *Bunty* (1958–2001) and *Judy* launched in 1960, priced at 4½d. The first weekly issue of *Diana* appeared on 23 February 1963, cost 6d and had a free gift of a golden chain bracelet inside. Magazines like *Honey* (1960–86), *Petticoat* (1966–75) and *Jackie* (1962–93) were aimed specifically at teenage girls.

As the kit modelling hobby grew in the 1960s, Airfix, founded in 1939, expanded its range to include vintage and modern cars, motorcycles, figures, trains, track-side accessories, military vehicles, large classic ships, warships, liners, engines, rockets and spaceships, as well as an ever-increasing range of aircraft.

although middle-class families were beginning to share social activities, in working-class families husbands and wives operated in separate spheres, with the pub and working men's club bastions of refuge for men. In the home a wife could expect to do three-quarters of the housework, including childcare, averaging 18½ hours a week.

Giving birth was still a daunting experience, and was an area in which the National Childbirth Trust, established as a charity in 1961, took an active interest, including lobbying government against excessive interventionist techniques, and encouraging husbands to attend antenatal classes and the actual birth. Popular names in 1964 included Susan, Tracey and Sharon, David, Paul and Richard. Many mothers relied upon Dr Benjamin Spock's best-selling *Common Sense Book of Baby and Child Care*, which advocated a less rigid approach to child rearing, encouraging affection and parental common sense.

Most children enjoyed a good deal of freedom, Cheryl T recalled being able to 'pop next door in the '60s and leave your door open without worry of someone breaking in. We were allowed out to play and shouted back in for meals.' Even though Cheryl remembered making her own entertainment, toy manufacturers recorded remarkable sales as the retail market exploded in 1960, reaching £80 million that year. Lego made its first appearance at the inaugural British Toy and Hobby Fair that year and was an instant success, while Clackers and Space Hoppers were all the rage. One of the biggest attractions at the 1963 fair was the board game Diplomacy, but Matchbox also scored a hit with model die-cast cars that had opening doors. Other toys that did well during the decade were Scalextric, Fuzzy Felt and Airfix, but it was the television-themed toys that really captured the market. The *Dr Who* television series created a huge demand for Dalek-themed toys and in 1965 the BBC issued licenses for ninety products ranging from clockwork Dalek models to astro-ray Dalek guns. In 1966 Action

A selection of 1960s toys, games and ephemera.

Man caused a sensation as the first boy's doll in the UK, and 1967 saw the launch of Etch-a-Sketch. Girls, already captivated by the Barbie doll, created in the USA in 1959, were able to feed their fantasy of a modelling career like that of Lesley Hornby – aka Twiggy, the world's first supermodel – with the launch, by Mattel, of the Twiggy Barbie in 1967. Not to be outdone, British company Pedigree came up with a doll which epitomised the carefree girl about swinging London, complete with Mary Quant bob, pony and moped. The Sindy doll, with her 'girl next door' looks, was the best-selling toy in Britain in 1968, and won the coveted Toy of the Year award that year.

Teenagers had more liberty than their predecessors and many parents allowed them to come and go as they pleased. Most youngsters left school at fifteen and became part of the new youth culture with money to spend on clothes and music, and the chance to become part of the new politicised youth movements. But for teenagers in the north of England change came slowly, and they felt themselves 'behind the times', exemplified by one girl who said 'everything reached Hull about five years after it reached everywhere else.'

The notion that family life was all cosy and rosy in 1960s Britain was challenged by two BBC kitchen-sink drama documentaries. The first, in 1965, was *Up the Junction*, which portrayed slum living in Battersea, complete with petty thieves, back-street abortion and sexual encounters. The following year *Cathy Come Home* exposed how the inflexible nature of the welfare system led to Cathy losing her home, her husband and eventually her child. This had a powerful impact on wider society, and precipitated huge support for a new charity, Shelter, launched on 1 December 1966, which campaigned to end homelessness and bad housing.

Most families took holidays together and for Shawn Fairless of Newcastle, a seaside trip was a mammoth outing for it included him, his parents, two grandparents and two siblings, cousins, aunts, uncles and neighbours. As a teenager, Julie Wood from Middlesborough travelled with her family to 'exotic' places like

Car ownership had a powerful democratising effect for it enabled people to travel further afield and experience places they had previously only read about. It also fuelled the British love affair with caravanning, giving a huge boost to the home industry as well as increasing the Caravan Club's membership, which doubled during the course of the decade.

Cornwall, the Lake District and Scotland for their annual summer caravan and camping vacation. Everything was packed in the Cortina or Mini, the roof rack was laden with cooking utensils and

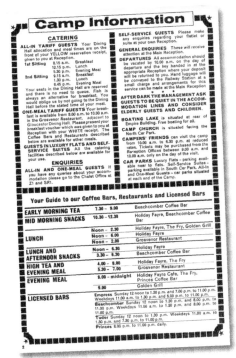

Entertainment brochure for Butlin's Skegness, September 1969.

Butlin's Skegness originally opened in 1936. Self-catering flatlets were added in the 1960s as well as a chairlift, a monorail and miniature railway, with two full-size ex-British Railways steam locomotives on display inside the loop.

BUTLIN'S SKEGNESS
General View showing Heated Pool

25

clothes, and the awning for the caravan was rammed in the trailer. But the best part of every holiday was the bacon her dad fried for breakfast on a primus stove. This was definitely not on the menu at kosher hotels like the Green Park and The Ambassadors in Bournemouth, which attracted Jewish families from all over the country. There they spent their summer holidays enjoying cricket and football matches, putting, table tennis, and swimming, as well as enjoying the all-important food.

While adventurous motorists and passengers crossed the Channel by ferry or on the new hovercraft to France and beyond, tooting other cars with a GB sticker in a spirit of camaraderie, cheaper air travel had an impact on British holiday habits. Domestic

air travel doubled from one million passenger kilometres in 1961 to two million passenger kilometres in 1971, many of them as part of the new all-inclusive package holiday. Between 1960 and 1961 nearly 500,000 Britons took package holidays, compared with 40,000 in 1953–54, and in 1962 Thomson's first organised foreign trip departed from Manchester to Palma, Spain, with eighty passengers on a thirteen-day trip which cost 41 guineas. Butlin's and Pontins responded to the loss of business by tempting holiday camp devotees to their new continental counterparts, with little success. For those who could not afford to fly, a visit to London's Heathrow airport and its roof gardens was the next best thing, and every year some 800,000 people did just that.

This B170 at Lydd Airport carried up to three cars with up to fourteen passengers and a flight attendant in the rear cabin. In January 1963 Silver City Airways and Channel Air Bridge merged to become British United Air Ferries.

# Exotic Beef Curry & Rice in 15 minutes
## prepared by Vesta for you to cook

ique sauce recipe gives authentic flavour to this true Indian-style Beef Curry.
complete: exotic and delicious beef curry, Vesta top quality Patna rice, all
you to cook in 15 minutes.

chefs have done the hard work for you: chopped the lean beef, prepared the
pples and tomatoes, blended the subtle, spicy curry sauce. *You* simply pop
e saucepan . . . and take the credit for cooking a meal fit for a prince!

Serves One 1/11d    Serves Two 3/3d

*Other adventurous di*

# VEST

VEGETABLE CURRY W
CHOW MEIN WITH CRISP
SPAGHETTI BOLOG

# FOOD AND DRINK

L IKE SO MANY OTHER ASPECTS of 1960s life, the food and drink altered dramatically, with the opportunities to try and buy a wider range of products gradually tempting even the most conservative eaters. Families generally sat down to meals together, and, as Cheryl T recalled, 'ate what was put in front of us'. For ordinary people, Sunday lunch – called dinner if you lived in the north-east like Kate G – was the most important meal of the week. A roast chicken or a joint of meat with potatoes and fresh vegetables would be stretched to provide other meals. Many families ate fish on Fridays, salads were dressed with Heinz salad cream, and olive oil was still 'medicinal' and sold at the chemist shop. Not only was bottled milk delivered to the door every day, but a weekly visit from the Corona van brought glass, returnable bottles of flavoured fizzy drinks, including Cherryade and Cream Soda, to households across the country. A smaller company, Jaycon, operated across London. The new self-service supermarkets stocked produce flown in from abroad, introducing out-of-season vegetables like tomatoes from the Canary Islands in winter, as well as avocado pears and exotic fruits. Travel abroad gave people a taste for herbs and spices, garlic and parsley, and the Mediterranean influence soon caught on. Dried pasta was a great novelty, and the sight of long, stiff strands of spaghetti being fed into a pan of boiling water astonished one young woman in 1964, for she had only previously seen or tasted tinned spaghetti. New immigrants from the Commonwealth, Uganda and Kenya introduced the population to curries, but home efforts were not always successful. The first time Margaret Maudsley of Blackpool tried her hand at curry-making she put so much curry powder in that everything turned yellow, including her curtains. The traditional loaf of bread was challenged in 1961 with the invention of the Chorleywood process, which produced the hugely popular, longer-lasting white sliced loaf. In 1966 a large loaf cost 1s 3½d, and the small size was 9d, while the English butter to spread on

Opposite:
Vesta ready-made curries first appeared in 1961.

29

it was 4s 5d per pound. Fridges allowed for safer and longer storage of perishable goods, including cooked or uncooked meat and poultry, and sales of both increased to unprecedented levels, with 150 million chickens eaten in 1965 alone. And what better place to keep your food fresh than in one of the American-made Tupperware plastic containers with the unique re-sealable lid, which were being sold at Tupperware parties from 1960. Ski seized the opportunity to introduce new fruit-flavoured yoghurts, marketed as 'the full-of-fitness' food, and Bird's launched Angel Delight, in strawberries and cream flavour in 1967.

More sugar – costing 1s 5d for 2 pounds in 1966 – was consumed than ever before, probably in reaction to the years of rationing, and much of it found its way onto new sugar-coated cereals, into children's sweet cigarettes – which were still being sold despite the ban on the TV advertising of cigarettes after 1965 – and chocolate bars like Topic in 1962, Toffee Crisp in 1963 and Twix and Marathon in 1967. The 'go to work on an egg' campaign, launched in 1957, peaked in the 1960s as UK egg consumption reached five per person per week. Even though domestic freezers were still a luxury, with only a third of homes owning one at the end of the decade, frozen food became increasingly popular. Frozen chips went on sale for the first time in the 1960s and 'Captain Birds Eye' became a familiar figure on television from 1967, while Birds Eye peas were renowned for being 'fresh as the moment when the pod went pop'. But the one slogan that was more successful than any others was 'Beanz Meanz Heinz', first used in 1967. Bejam – the pioneering shop devoted to frozen food – opened

A family in the 1960s enjoying an array of Easter eggs including Cadbury's Milk Tray, Rowntree's, Mackintosh's and Quality Street.

in Stanmore, Middlesex in 1968, and even Harrods had its own-label variety of frozen fish and chips, which continued to be the nation's favourite meal. Catchy jingles accompanying television adverts successfully persuaded housewives to purchase their products. Baking could benefit from Cookeen margarine which 'gives you the golden touch', while McDougall's flour was 'super-sifted'. Once Cadbury introduced their instant potato – Smash – housewives were also relieved of the need to peel, boil and mash.

By the end of the decade more than £19 million was being spent every year on slimming and starch-reduced products, with Limmits and Trimmets joining other ranges in the 1960s. New low-calorie soft drinks made with improved artificial sweeteners proved popular, while some £12 million passed through the tills of health food shops annually, as people bought wholemeal bread, free-range eggs and compost-grown vegetables from them, mostly because they preferred the taste. Entertaining at home gave the adventurous cook the opportunity to broaden their culinary skills, and impress their guests. Many continued to turn to the flamboyant Fanny Cradock and her hen-pecked partner Johnnie – it only transpired after they had retired from television that they were not married – for advice, but for gourmet food no one did more to change the domestic dinner party

This seventy-two-part weekly series provided home cooks with a step-by-step Cordon Bleu cookery course.

than American-born Robert Carrier. His *Great Dishes of the World*, first serialised in *The Sunday Times* colour supplement in 1962, and his innovative packs of cookery cards introduced tens of thousands of middle-class women to continental recipes which used cream, butter and brandy. To complete the meal there were After Eight Mints or Matchmakers, and taking a leaf from the Continent, informed hostesses rejected sweet white Liebfraumilch and instead chose a dry white wine or pink Mateus Rosé. Wine consumption nearly doubled between 1960 and 1969, from an average 3.6 pints of wine a year to nearly 7 pints by 1969 per person, while the quantity of beer consumed rose from 18.9 gallons per head per year in 1960 to 22.6 gallons a decade later. Strongbow, launched in 1962, epitomised the sporty, active image of cider's growing market of young consumers. Lager, which began to be brewed in Britain in the 1960s, appealed to women and young drinkers far more than mild or bitter, and along

TV cook Fanny Cradock, tasting her latest creation with pupil cook John Harper (centre) and partner Johnnie, 28 October 1962.

with the new carbonated and pasteurised 'keg' draught, was ideal for canning, and for sale in supermarkets.

For the growing number of people who wanted to eat out, the early 1960s were rather a wasteland, but there were rapid changes afoot both at the popular and upper end of the market, as new enterprises sprang up all over the country. The contribution made by immigrants was huge, with the number of Indian restaurants – especially appealing as they stayed open later than the pubs – increasing from 500 in 1960 to over 1,200 a decade later. The Good Friends in Salmon Lane, east London was just one of the many Chinese restaurants and takeaways which opened up in almost every large and medium-sized town in England. Pekinese food arrived with the opening of Mr Kuo's restaurant, Kuo Yuan, in 1963, introducing north-west Londoners and other intrepid travellers to Peking duck and the ritual of pancake rolling. For conventional tastes a meal of steak and chips, a glass of red wine followed by an Irish coffee at a Berni Inn, first opened in 1956, became the highlight of the week for many, and at its peak in the 1960s the firm was opening a new restaurant every month. When the Mill Inn at Withington, Gloucestershire experimented with fried chicken in a basket one bank

Young men drinking at the Black Bull, The Rock, Bury, Lancashire, c. 1966. After they had finished they would go the local record shop and listen to a few tracks of the latest hits.

The views from the revolving restaurant at the top of the 600-foot-high glass and steel Post Office Tower were spectacular. However, the food was not, and failed to get a place in Egon Ronay's prestigious restaurant guide.

*The high life.*

*Superb wines, excellent food and beneath and around you... London.*
*See the Panorama of London from 520 feet up at London's only revolving restaurant.*
*London by day for luncheons.*
*London by night for dinners and after theatre suppers. The Top of the Tower Restaurant is open 7 days a week. Parties up to 80 accepted.*
*Midweek reservations are immediately available.*
*Dial 01-636 3000 to reserve your table.*
*Then watch the world go round.*

**topofthetower restaurant**
*Maple Street. W1*
*The Butlin Group of Companies*

holiday weekend, they had no idea how popular the dish would become as people travelled miles to enjoy this novel meal. Moderately priced establishments expanded their operations, exemplified by the Little Chef chain of roadside restaurants, which grew from one branch in Reading opening in 1958, to twelve branches nationwide by 1965, including one in London's Hyde Park. By 1968 there were twenty-five of these American-style diners scattered across the country. Even more successful was the Wimpy Bar chain, which had more than 1,000 branches serving fast-food hamburgers in the UK by the end of the 1960s, with nine in Oxford Street alone. The first Kentucky Fried Chicken shop arrived in Preston, Lancashire in 1965, the same year as Pizza Express opened its first branch in Soho. Cranks, the first truly vegetarian restaurant, opened in Carnaby Street, Soho in 1961, well before the street became part of Swinging London. Diners flocked to Butlin's Top of the Tower restaurant on the thirty-sixth floor of the new Post Office Tower after it was inaugurated by Harold Wilson on 8 October 1965.

Meanwhile, thousands of schoolchildren participated in a quite different dining experience as they faced their school dinner each day. For Rowena, they were characterised by the 'never to be forgotten' aroma of boiled cabbage, while another pupil recalled 'boiled potatoes like bullets, with black bits on the skin and steamed puddings with watery custard and skin on top'. All this for 1s, until the price increased to 1s 6d in 1968.

Britain may have been a predominantly tea-drinking nation, but coffee bars gained in popularity and became a popular haunt for the new teenagers, with 2,000 across the country, including 500 in Greater London and 200 in the West End alone in 1960. Newcastle had, among others, The Palletta, where girls like Jane Boyd listened to records on the jukebox and made a coffee last all afternoon. Bar Italia in Frith Street, Soho, was a favoured haunt for Mods and their Lambrettas, but there was competition from the Golden Egg venues, which were renowned for their riotous colour schemes and varied continental themes, their coffee and reasonably priced food.

The first Pizza Express restaurant opened on Wardour Street, Soho, in 1965, promising authentic Italian-style food and live jazz.

THIS IS SWINGING LONDON

MICK JA

City of Westminster
CARNABY
ST. W.1

City of Westmins
PICCADILLY
CIRCUS W.1

POW

HAROLD

YOU

TWIG

KING'S
ROAD

LK 55

# SHOPPING AND FASHION

THE NEWLY AFFLUENT society wanted to shop, and with a 130 per cent growth in average weekly earnings between 1955 and 1969, they had money to spend. Launching on 29 June 1966, Barclaycard was the first all-purpose credit card scheme to be operated by a British bank. Credit limits were set at £100 and £200 and from 8 November 1967 Barclaycard became the first credit card to offer extended credit, effectively a mini-overdraft facility. Interest was charged at 1.5 per cent each month on the balance left twenty-five days after the statement was issued. Chain stores, including Boots, F. W. Woolworth and Marks and Spencer, enjoyed an unprecedented growth in popularity and profit in the 1960s, and accounted for 28 per cent of all retail sales, a figure that had increased to 37 per cent by 1971. Food shopping was transformed with the advent of the supermarket – the number of stores increasing from 367 in 1960 to nearly 3,000 by 1967. Tesco opened in Cheltenham in 1960 with an unprecedented 4,200 square feet of selling space with Morrison's not far behind with their first supermarket in Bradford in 1961. The company converted a cinema to create 5,000 square feet of retail space selling fresh meat, greengrocery and other provisions. By 1968 Tesco had coined the term 'superstore' for a new shop in Crawley with 40,000 square feet. Meanwhile, Sainsbury became the first food retailer to computerise distribution in 1961. They were quick to tailor products to local tastes and introduced Chinese ingredients into their Bristol store in 1961, and the following year led the way in acquiring an off-licence, a trend which other supermarkets soon adopted. The number of Sainsbury's food products doubled to 4,000 over the course of the decade, and by 1969 their own brand lines accounted for 50 per cent of turnover. Woolworth launched their own label Winfield products in 1963. Price competition was a new phenomenon, brought about by the Resale Prices Act of

Opposite: This souvenir poster, c. 1969, produced for the Carnaby Street boutique 'I was Lord Kitchener's Valet', featured a series of cartoons symbolising Britain and fashionable London pop culture. These included Mick Jagger, Prince Charles, Lord Kitchener, Harold Wilson, the Houses of Parliament and Twiggy, the world's first supermodel.

1964, which abolished resale price maintenance. As the big retailers vied for custom, competing trading stamps appeared as an incentive to attract shoppers with their promise of free gifts.

Frequent trips to the local shops, like those that Andrea M's mother did twice a week in Fairwater, Cardiff, 'where the goods would be chosen for her by the shopkeeper', were increasingly replaced by weekly visits to the new emporia, prompting Andrea, in Ilfracombe, Devon, to remark, in 1968, 'How strange it was to push the wire trolley around and to hunt on shelves for what we wanted!' There were shops that defied change, like B. B. Evans, a well-known independent department store in Kilburn, north London, which continued to use a vacuum system of cartridges and tubes for payments in the mid-1960s. Outdoors, the popularity of gardening and the advent of containerised plants gave the impetus to new local purpose-built garden centres, with Gardenlands at Christchurch, Dorset the first to open its doors in October 1961.

As the new consumers clamoured for the latest trends, designers were ready to feed their fantasies, and London became a mecca for everything fashionable. Newly affluent middle-class couples in their

twenties and thirties were able to buy into a new lifestyle at Terence Conran's shop Habitat which opened in Fulham Road, an unfashionable part of Chelsea, in May 1964. From the beginning, Habitat displayed living rooms and kitchens in store, selling everything from pine furnishings to pots and pans, and innovatively, had customers wandering around, picking up items at their leisure. Even the female shop assistants were stylish, for they were encouraged to have Vidal Sassoon-style bobbed haircuts and wear the latest Mary Quant dresses. Both Quant and Sassoon played an important part in liberating women. His radical, geometric hairstyles released them from the tyranny of the hair lacquer spray, the hooded hair dryer and hair rollers. Her mini-skirts, named after her favourite car, freed women from hobble skirts and corsets, and allowed them to run for a bus. Tights, which she claimed to have invented, replaced stockings and suspenders, but whether you wore them under or over knickers perplexed many girls. The King's Road in Chelsea, where Quant opened her second branch of Bazaar in 1963, became a mecca for the stylish 'Chelsea Set', and local

Loyalty schemes like Green Shield and S & H Stamps became a hugely popular customer incentive, even though dozens of books filled with stamps were required for the free gift. Each book of Green Shield Stamps contained 1,280 stamps, one for every 6d spent. In 1965 gifts available for a complete book included a set of six mugs, six lager glasses with gold rims and a gent's brush and comb set.

The Co-operative, like this branch at 90 Windmill Hill, Cradley, maintained customer loyalty with their own saver stamps.

residents looked on in amazement at their floppy hats, skinny ribbed sweaters, key-hole dresses, wide hipster belts, Op-Art earrings and ankle-length white boots. By 1965, when hemlines had risen to nearly 6 inches above the knee, Quant had launched a wholesale clothes label, 'The Ginger Group', and was designing make-up, providing 'everything you need for the look of the moment', all packaged with her signature daisy logo. Her last big fashion development, hot pants, came at the end of the 1960s. By then Biba had become the trendiest London boutique, and the model Twiggy, born Lesley Hornby in north London in 1949, was named 'the face of '66' by the *Daily Express*. The original supermodel, she enjoyed international success before retiring from modelling in 1969 to pursue a film career. Boys sported Beatle haircuts and wore winkle picker shoes, and favoured shops on King's Road and Carnaby

Vidal Sassoon
cutting a client's
hair at Dingles,
Plymouth, Devon,
1960s.

New shopping
centres, like
Birmingham's Bull
Ring, with its novel
ring road system,
were of a unique
design and took
practice to master.

The Triumph Herald car was a favourite with young people, here pictured outside Mary Quant's shop, Bazaar, on Brompton Road, 1967.

**MARY QUANT · BAZAAR · 46 BROMPTON ROAD · LONDON S·W·3·**

Miners cosmetics were at the lower end of the price range and produced up-to-the-minute make-up in high fashion colours, favoured by Mods.

## Miners has it:

Nude Look. For nails. Called Supernaturals. 8 near-naked supercolours you can see right through. Only Miners has them. In Creamy Natural, Creamy Pink, Creamy Candy, Creamy Beige, Creamy Tan, Natural, Clear and White Out. 1/10. Frosteds too. 2/8.

Miners has it all. For eyes. Lips. Nails. Hair. All the new things. Always.

**m** THE SHAKE-UP IN MAKE-UP

Street. They could choose from Lord John and I was Lord Kitchener's Valet, or visit Harry Fenton, John Michael and John Stephen, where, in 1966, you could buy a suit for 37 guineas and a gold lamé leather jacket for 50 guineas. On the high street Etam, Wallis, Richard Shops, Chelsea Girl and Top Shop were trendy places to shop, and newly developed easy-care polyester, nylon and crimplene were popular fabrics. University students had their own dress code that, for men, included grubby jeans and a black leather jacket.

*Honey*, the first fashion magazine for young women, was published in April 1960 and by October had the tag line 'for the teens and twenties.' For high fashion Mods, make up was defining, characterised by pale skin and 'panda eyes', achieved by applying dark eyeliner and lots of mascara producing spiky eyelashes. Jane George-John remembered going to Woolworth's to buy their 'flavoured lipstick that came in pink, red, orange or beige, and gold nail polish that looked like nicotine stains'.

Opposite: Ladies trying on hats in the millinery department of British Home Stores, Oxford Street, London c. 1960s.

# HOME AND
# NEIGHBOURHOOD

THE 1960S WITNESSED SLUM CLEARANCE programmes, which swept away derelict and not-so-derelict nineteenth-century homes across the country from Newcastle to Sheffield, Birmingham to Bradford. In their place came a further generation of new towns like Harlow, Essex, which had so many young families with prams and pushchairs that it earned the nickname 'Pram Town'. Council estates were built on the outskirts of cities, miles away from work, shops and friends, and high-rise flats sprang up, sowing the seeds for broken communities. These tower blocks, including T. Dan Smith's Cruddas Park in Newcastle, were heralded as the solution to the housing crisis, but out-of-order lifts left the elderly and those with children stranded, while the freedom to play on the street, under the watchful eye of a parent close by, was increasingly eroded the higher up the block a family lived. Many people, like Dolly Lloyd, whose house was one of many demolished around Kirby and Scotland Road in Liverpool, simply did not want to 'live up there', but was 'persuaded by the promise of a verandah with a garden below, and the luxury of a bathroom'. Tower blocks failed to solve the accommodation crisis and in September 1969 Shelter estimated that there were up to three million people in Britain urgently needing re-housing because they were living in damp, overcrowded slum conditions, often paying exorbitant rents imposed by unscrupulous landlords. This was despite the 1965 Rent Act, which introduced rent officers and tribunals, and also partially restored rent controls, which had been deregulated by the 1957 Act. The crisis precipitated the founding, by Reverend Kenneth Leech, of the housing charity, Centrepoint, which opened its first shelter for homeless youngsters in a Soho church in December 1969.

Before gas fires and central heating, homes were almost universally cold, with warmth provided by paraffin heaters and coal fires. The coal man, and coal bunkers outside the back door, were familiar sights. Frost on the inside of bedroom windows was commonplace, and was

Opposite:
Ronan Point being prepared for demolition. The gas explosion that destroyed an entire corner of Ronan Point – a brand-new 200-foot-high, twenty-two-storey 110-flat block – in east London on 16 May 1968, not only killed four people and injured seventeen, but shattered people's confidence in high-rise homes.

Back-to-back houses in Bolton in the 1960s, where the children played on the street and mothers left babies in their prams outside the front door.

something that Paul Cobb remembered, particularly during the freezing winter of 1962–63. For six-year-old Janet M, 1963 was indelibly etched on her mind for her family moved from a spotlessly clean Glasgow tenement to an 'incredibly modern' post-war pre-fab, which, besides having a bathroom with a hot-air linen cupboard had 'two bedrooms, a living/dining room' and 'a fitted "metal" kitchen with gas fridge'. This family were among the 33 per cent of households in the early 1960s with a refrigerator, a figure that rose to 69 per cent by 1971. The metal kitchen units were superseded by Hygena's pioneering Formica, the new easy-to-clean material used for door panels and worktops. 'Must-have' labour saving devices, made possible by revolutionary technology, included vacuum cleaners, dishwashers and washing machines. Of varying quality, these were as likely to be found in middle-class houses as they were in the homes of the poorest people in the St Ann's district of Nottingham. These poor folk were exactly the market targeted by the entrepreneur John Bloom, whose company promised to bring 'luxury Rolls Domestic Appliances…within the reach of thousands of housewives at a price they could afford.' Buying goods on the 'never-

never' or hire purchase made them attractive and by the end of 1963 the Rolls Razor company was selling over 200,000 machines a year. Bloom quickly became a millionaire, but his luck ran out as his competitors launched a price-cutting campaign. His company went into liquidation in 1964 and Bloom was subsequently prosecuted for a variety of offences including fraud, but escaped with a fine of £30,000.

When it came to furnishing the home, Scandinavian designs, in teak especially, grew in popularity, with British mass-market manufacturers including Archie Shine, Ercol, and Stag producing merchandise in competition with foreign imports. Stag's existing Minstrel range in African cherry wood, revamped by designers John and Sylvia Reid, was a modern take on eighteenth-century design, and became one of the

The Kenwood Chef, with its large range of attachments, became an iconic piece of kitchen equipment. The new Sheer Look, designed by Kenneth Grange in 1960, was voted 'the British housewife's all-time favourite kitchen appliance'.

A dining-room setting from Ercol's 1965 catalogue featuring the solid elm and beech Windsor latticed chair and solid elm serving cabinet with drop-down flap.

47

These early 1960s tea and coffee pots, designed by Susan William Ellis for Portmeirion Pottery, were too popular for their own good, and were easily copied with cheaper versions. Left to right, Cypher, Totem and Jupiter.

best-selling ranges of furniture of all time. But for cutting-edge design, nowhere could beat Habitat, which brought contemporary design – bright colours, clean lines and natural woods – to the high street, and to an affluent generation of middle-class baby boomers. To complete this, Peter Blake and David Hockney produced Pop Art pictures, while Bridget Riley's black and white Op Art paintings became synonymous with everything that was modern, young and sophisticated. Many people now aspired to own their own homes, with the proportion of owners in the country rising from 37 per cent

'Baroque', a late 1960s design by Jessie Tait for Midwinter Pottery.

At its height in the mid-1960s, Cyril Lord was employing 4,000–5,000 people, and was a household name. When the company went into receivership in November 1968, it had debts of £7 million, and was one of the most highly publicised corporate failures since the end of the Second World War.

in 1959 to 44 per cent in 1964. In 1960 the average cost of a home was £2,507 with Yorkshire and Humberside the region with the lowest prices. Anne L and her husband discussed the possibility soon after they married in 1960, and despite her reservations, he insisted they save up to buy a place of their own, with the help of an aunt who loaned them the deposit money in 1962. Having your own telephone was still a luxury in the 1960s, with many people unable to get more than a shared line. It was 1965 before the old alphanumeric phone numbers – WHItehall 1212 was Scotland Yard

F. W. Woolworth was selling furniture, and much more, at its first Woolco superstore in Oadby, Leicester in 1967. It had 63,000 square feet of selling space on a single floor and was a one-stop shop for the whole family.

– were replaced with all-number codes, and at the end of the decade half of all households were still without a phone.

By the early 1960s four out of five British homes had a garden, and this neat suburban space was both a haven and a place on which to spend money. Gardening became a hugely popular pastime, and Percy Thrower's *Gardening Club* and *Gardener's World* on BBC television attracted huge audiences. Lawn-mowing was revolutionised with the Swedish-designed Flymo, the battery-operated 'hover-mower' launched in 1965, and by the electric version, a world first, in 1969. Indoors, the new do-it-yourself enthusiast could follow Barry Bucknell's expert advice on the BBC, read a specialist publication like *Practical Householder Magazine*, or visit the Ideal Home Exhibition in London, which attracted 1,128,123 people in 1965.

The character of neighbourhoods altered as immigrants from the West Indies, India, Pakistan and elsewhere arrived in cities including Birmingham, Nottingham, Wolverhampton and London, raising racial resentment. This came as a shock to the broadcaster Darcus Howe when he arrived at Waterloo Station from Trinidad in April 1962, aged nineteen. His friend warned him never to walk alone at night because he would face arrest by the police and a beating from white racists, and he seriously thought about turning around and going home immediately. He did stay, but had his world turned upside down when the election campaign took place in the Midlands county borough of Smethwick in 1964. To be confronted by slogans including 'If you want a nigger for a neighbour, vote Liberal or Labour', was bad enough, but it was Enoch Powell's speech in 1968, which Darcus recalled 'threatened us with rivers of blood and painted the imagery of the Tiber foaming with our blood' that shook him to the core. He repeatedly begged his parents to send him a ticket to go home and although they were sympathetic, they pleaded with him to stick it out. Others, like Frank Collins, experienced racism at a more mundane level: when he was looking for somewhere to live in London in 1967 he was confronted by advertisements in newsagent windows which stated 'No Irish, no blacks need apply'. He counted himself very lucky to find 'a very good English family to let me rent one of their rooms. My age was twenty years and it was the first time I was away from home, in another country.'

Lawnmowers and other gardening equipment on sale at the Woolco superstore, Leicester.

# EDUCATION AND SOCIAL SERVICES

EDUCATION underwent great changes in the 1960s, especially towards the end of the decade. The 1967 Plowden Report recommended a child-centred approach to primary education, and advocated the expansion of mainly part-time nursery provision, and at the same time selection at secondary level was being challenged and the growth of university and polytechnics got underway. Personal social services, which provided care and support for the most vulnerable in society – pensioners, of whom there were 2.5 million in 1960, the physically and mentally handicapped, children and problem families – were the Cinderella services, and while the total annual public expenditure on social service benefits rose from £1,675,000 in 1961–62 to £2,642,000 in 1966–67, they were poorly funded with only 1.7 per cent of public expenditure apportioned to them in 1966.

In the early 1960s there were no state pre-schools or nurseries, so most children were five years old before they started infant or primary school, with a bi-annual intake in February and September. Stepps Primary School in Scotland took a flexible approach, placing youngsters, like Fiona Middler, whose mother had taught her to read and write at home, in the older age group, with another child she knew. In 1964, three-quarters of primary school teachers were women, and while pupil numbers in schools averaged around 188 throughout the decade, there were exceptions. Longmeadow in Hertfordshire, for example, had 350 children on the infant register in January 1960, and admitted forty-one five-year-olds that February. Many of the buildings, including those of Western Junior in North Shields, were cold and draughty, relics of the Victorian era, with huge windows that could only be opened by using a hooked stick. Some had outmoded facilities and Sue of Lincoln recalled the 'scary toilets with fixed wooden seats and high level cisterns with deafening flushes'.

Opposite:
The children from Cheriton Fitzpaine primary school, Crediton, Devon watching the roof of their seventeenth-century school building being re-thatched in the early 1960s. Located in the oldest thatch longhouse in the village, the school was started in 1875.

Miss Chalmers' class at Longmeadow Infants School giving a gym display on parents' afternoon, June 1961. There was no proper gym kit so the children wore their vests, knickers or underpants and bare feet or pumps, which were usually purchased from Woolworth's.

Other schools, like the one Yvonne B attended, had 'lovely, cosy coal fires and kind, patient teachers', and she was devastated when slum clearance swept it away, replacing it with 'a massive new school filled with strange, hostile faces'. When snow fell from the end of December 1963 until March 1964 schools were regularly closed and children sent home.

Day-to-day life at primary and junior school fell into a predictable routine, with the teacher standing at the front of the class and the children sitting at desks facing the board. 'The Three Rs' – reading, writing and arithmetic – were very important, learning by rote was the norm, with times tables chanted aloud in class, and poetry memorised for homework. Neat handwriting was practised daily, and nature study was often the only science taught at primary school. In school halls up and down the country children took part in 'Singing Together' or 'Music and Movement', transmitted on the radio by the School Broadcasting Council, and could be found leaping and stretching to the commands: 'Now children we are going to sway like trees in the wind.' Jenny Armes remembered playtime at Middle Street Primary, Brighton in the early 1960s, where, like children up and down the country, she played 'jacks', French skipping and hula hoops, or bounced balls against the wall on a length of elastic, and lots of other fads'. But for one girl at Western Infant School, North Tyneside in 1963, climbing on the coke heap during a break resulted in a smack on the top of the leg by a female teacher, a punishment which was worth it as 'that coke heap was just too interesting to ignore!' Corporal punishment lingered in primary schools until well after the Plowden Report, *Children and Primary Schools* (1967), which besides condemning the practice also came out against rote learning and drill. Break time was characterised by the bottle of free milk, delivered in crates to school gates across the country every morning, and left outside until required. Frozen milk was defrosted on the radiator in winter ending up watery and lukewarm, and in summer it curdled and separated out. But there was no leaving it, as the teacher would say 'milk is good for you child, you WILL drink it all up!' Wilson's Labour government withdrew the facility for children at secondary school in 1968.

Aerial view of the newly built Downs Secondary Modern School at Compton, near Newbury in Berkshire in 1961/2. It was built as a two-form entry school with capacity for around 350, but started with 275–300 pupils.

55

G.C.E. RESULTS.    ORDINARY LEVEL.
ENGLISH LANGUAGE    1    pass    Distinction.
ENGLISH LITERATURE    5    pass
HISTORY    5    pass
FRENCH    6.2    pass
CHEMISTRY    8    failure
BIOLOGY    3    pass
PURE MATHEMATICS A.    2    pass.

Pupils at Woodford County High School, an all-girls grammar school, left a self-addressed postcard at school, which was then posted to them with their General Certificate of Education graded 'O' Level results. This card was received in August 1961.

Secondary-level state education for the 3.2 million pupils in the United Kingdom in the early 1960s was divided between grammar schools and secondary modern, with two in every three state-educated twelve-year-olds attending the latter in 1960. There were a further 410,000 pupils in recognised independent and direct grant grammar schools and 195,000 in other independent schools in 1961.

Middle-class parents in particular considered the secondary modern inferior and the route to nowhere, especially not university. No wonder then that Kath Checkland and her sister, who took their eleven-plus in the late 1960s, spent every day of their final year in their 'middle-class-dominated and aspirational primary school learning to pass the eleven-plus.' The training worked: against a national pass rate of 25 per cent her school achieved approximately 75 per cent success. Less successful was Andrew P, who ended up in the bottom stream at Dunsmore Secondary School for Boys in 1965, having been written off as a lost cause. He spent his days there doing metalwork and woodwork and smoking Players No. 6 behind the bike sheds. Even though grammar school offered bright working-class children the opportunity of social mobility, some communities, like the one Paul Bolsover lived in, considered it very elitist, and there was scorn and derision hurled at anyone who passed the exam and went there. Despite the Labour government's efforts at ending the segregation of children in separate schools, abolishing the eleven-plus exam and reorganising secondary schools on comprehensive lines, there was no compulsion for local authorities to comply, so the selection process continued in many places, including the London boroughs of Barnet and Woodford. The school-leaving age remained at fifteen throughout the 1960s, but was raised to sixteen in the 1970s, as recommended by the Newsom Report, *Half Our Future*, published in 1963.

As a result of the post-war baby boom there were 600,000 young people aged eighteen in 1963, and with more of them wanting to go on to university, tertiary education was reorganised and expanded. Admission depended on results of the Ordinary Level and Advanced Level General Certificate of Education exams, taken at sixteen and eighteen. The number of universities more than doubled from twenty to sixty-three, and included many new institutions, of which the University of Sussex, designed by Sir Basil Spence, was the first. By 1969 the University of Keele, awarded its Royal Charter in 1962, was being described as 'the most original innovation in British university education in the 20th century', but what remained largely unchanged was the demography of the student population, which was more than 75 per cent male. Despite this disproportion, the Anderson Committee, which reported in 1960 on the question of student grants, argued against any differentiation between the right of girls and boys to mandatory student grants, suggesting that it would be a mistake to try to measure the benefits of a university education solely in terms of earning capacity. A national system was recommended whereby every first-time undergraduate was eligible for a grant towards tuition fees and maintenance, the actual level of grant depending on student income. For Lawrence of Southampton, one of the nearly 70 per cent of students receiving a grant, this amounted to £12 per term in the early 1960s. Grants enabled more young people to choose universities away from home. Students at Oxford and Cambridge secured what was in effect a double subsidy from public funds, since both the university and their college fees were paid for them. The new universities offered innovative kinds of curricula in the arts, which proved especially attractive to women. Sociology became a major social science subject, and the University of Sussex pioneered school-based initial teacher training.

The library at the University of Sussex in c. 1963–66. The university expected to admit 200 from the 900 or so who applied for the first intake in 1962–63. As a result of the 1963 Robbins Report (the Committee on Higher Education) the university accelerated their planned total intake to 3,000, increasing this to 3,700 by 1967, and to 6,000 by 1977.

Most non-university higher education was reorganised into new technical universities and polytechnics, and over fifty existing technical and other colleges were combined into thirty institutions in a non-university, 'public' sector in order to address the increasing need for vocational, professional, and industrial-based courses that could not be met by the universities. The polytechnics, which had more than 150,000 students by 1973, were unlike the universities; they had more undergraduate than graduate students, more part-time students, and more 'sandwich' students, who combined work and study.

Besides funding the education system, the government were also financing the welfare state, at great cost. There were an estimated 6–9 per cent of the population in poverty in the 1960s, up to 29 per cent of whom were on the poverty line. The Child Poverty Action Group was established in 1965, in response to a claim that 720,000 children were living in poverty. There were also the homeless, the elderly, the unemployed, the mentally sick and more – a stark contrast to those enjoying the newly affluent and permissive society. The National Assistance Insurance Act came into force in 1961, introducing earnings-related pensions and contributions, and in 1966 the Social Security Act abolished national assistance, replacing it with supplementary benefits. The creation of the Department of Health and Social Security in 1968 brought the ministries of health, pensions and national insurance under one umbrella. As late as 1970, the weekly state pension was £5 for a single person and £8 2s for a married couple, which by any standards was inadequate. The survey *Sans Everything*, published in 1967, found deplorable conditions in both hospitals and homes for the elderly and disabled. The Committee on One Parent Families (Finer Committee) was established by Richard Crossman, secretary of state for social services, on 6 November 1969, to consider the problems of one-parent families and what help could be given them.

Princess Alice, Duchess of Gloucester, visiting the Southwark branch of the Invalid Meals for London service in New Kent Road, February 1960. Founded in 1910, this voluntary organisation was the forerunner of Meals on Wheels, and was taken over by the Greater London Council in 1961.

The Albemarle Committee, set up in 1958 to look at the problems of young people and state provision for them, reported to government in February 1960, and concluded that far more facilities, clubs and training were essential to prevent the real or imagined fear of a 'new climate of crime and delinquency.' Over the course of the decade some £28 million was spent on 3,000 building projects and the number of full-time youth workers doubled, while the Scouts enjoyed their highest ever UK membership of 557,918 in 1967.

A homeless man on the street. In direct contrast to 'Swinging London', Shelter reported in January 1966 that more than 12,000 people had seen in the New Year in a hostel for the homeless.

**D**
Stripy green/blue cape with shiny brass buttons, fastens over slightly-flared pants

**E**
Pixie-hooded twosome in whimsy lemon and coffee scattered cotton piqué

**J**
Joky carpenter's overall, zipped-up and buckled scooter-happy gaberdine

**K**
On the beat, traffic stopping green cape-suit, with naughty knickerbockers

**L**
On guard in two shades of pink suit. Battledress zipper jacket, side striped sleeves to match the pants

--- FREE ENTRY COUPON ---

## PETTICOAT Win-a-Scooter Competition

My order of choice for the eight Vespa Scootsuits is listed on the right. In entering the competition, I agree to the rules as final and legally binding.

NAME
(Mrs/Miss).................................

.................................................

ADDRESS...................................

.................................................

| | |
|---|---|
| 1st | |
| 2nd | |
| 3rd | |
| 4th | |
| 5th | |
| 6th | |
| 7th | |
| 8th | |

CUT OUT ROUND THIS LINE

# TRANSPORT

**B**RITAIN WAS TRULY ON THE MOVE, as the number of car owners doubled during the decade from 5.6 million to 11.8 million. Having a car was not only a symbol of affluence but also one of status. Four out of every five cars were made in Britain, keeping factories around the country busy, and striking new models – especially Alec Issigonis's 1959 Morris Mini-Minor, designed for the British Motor Corporation – became icons of the era. The small, stylish Mini had an affordable price tag ranging from £497 for the standard model to £606 for the deluxe automatic. The car was hugely successful, with some 510,000 Morris and 435,000 Austin Mk 1 saloon cars alone sold before the Mk 2 version was introduced in 1967. Paul Balcombe's standard turquoise-green Mini was a twenty-first birthday present in 1961, and was 'enhanced' by the straight-through exhaust he was persuaded to have fitted. The throaty noise from this was intended to turn the girls' heads but it did more than that when it unceremoniously fell off in Whitechapel High Street. There was an even greater racket when Paul jumped out of the car to pick up the box, completely forgetting it was red-hot. The Mini was joined in September 1960 by the Mini Traveller version with its distinctive wooden sideboards, at a price of £623, and sealed the Mini's reputation as the car for customers who wanted to be part of the new modern, mobile and active lifestyle. Equally distinctive, but aimed at a rather more affluent market, was the new E-type Jaguar which, when launched in 1961, cost over £2,200, including purchase tax and the all-important wire wheels. Ford's challenge in the burgeoning market was the Cortina, introduced in September 1962, which was advertised as 'the small car with a big difference', and had a price tag starting at £639 for a standard two-door version. Voted international car of the year at the 1964 Motor Show at Earl's Court, London, the mahogany dashboard and interior with leather seats so impressed one man

Opposite: The Vespa 90 was very popular with girls as well as boys, prompting *Petticoat* magazine to run a big fashion competition in April 1967, featuring eight Scoutsuits.

that he bought a silver 1600E on the spot. This was despite it earning the nickname of 'the Dagenham Dustbin' because it was very prone to rust. Cars in the 1960s were notoriously unreliable, and Julie Woods's father always kept a spare alternator in the boot, as well as a pair of her mother's tights in case the fan belt went. Shops like Andrew's Car Parts, which opened in north London in late 1962, were the answer to the trendy new car owner's dream, for they stocked everything that wasn't standard, including stick-on rear-screen heaters, fitted wirelesses for which you required a separate licence, and wing mirrors.

The cost of driving lessons varied across the country, with a man in Arbroath, Scotland recalling that in the mid-1960s he paid 'only' 15s an hour in a private car with no dual controls, or £1 an hour for a lesson in a dual-controlled vehicle. Sandra L paid rather more than that in London in 1964, forking out £1 2s 6d for her hour of tuition. Actually getting a licence in the 1960s was not easy, for more than 50 per cent of examinees, including Julian's father, failed the driving test. He could hardly have been surprised after knocking a village policeman off his bicycle during the first test, narrowly escaping a fine for dangerous driving before he had even passed! British motorists were lured by the promise of cheap car insurance in 1963, with the establishment of Fire, Auto and Marine Insurance by the self-styled Dr Emil Savundra, who for three years feathered his nest while customers waited for settlements to be made. When the company collapsed in June 1966 following published revelations of wrongdoing, there were 45,000 unsettled claims totalling more than £1.25 million and 400,000 customers left without insurance. Thanks to David Frost's skilful interviewing in February 1967, 'God's own lounge lizard turned swindler' as Savundra triumphantly called himself, was subsequently charged with fraud and sentenced to eight years' imprisonment and a fine of £50,000.

Ernest Marples, Conservative minister of transport until 16 October 1964, had already established the first 67-mile stretch of the M1 in 1959, setting the seal on the growth of motorways. Sections of the M60 and M6 were constructed between 1960 and 1963, with the first part of the A1(M) at Doncaster opened in 1961 and the first 2 miles of dual two-lane section of the M5 at Filton, near Bristol opened in 1962. The Road Traffic Act 1960 introduced the MOT test – initially for vehicles over ten years old and covering brakes, lights and steering – as well as measures to control how and where people parked their vehicles. Double-yellow lines joined the established single lines, and new on-street parking regulations in London from 19 September 1960 were enforced by traffic wardens. Dr Thomas Creighton was the first person in Britain to

Opposite: The forecourt of a garage, June 1968. The petrol pumps display nine different blends of petrol, from 92 to 100 Octane rating, ranging from 5s 4d to 6s a gallon. ESSO's 'Put a tiger in your tank' poster campaign was very successful. Many cars sported the campaign's bumper stickers, and 2.5 million people stuck comic tiger tails on their petrol caps.

A policeman on his Velocette in the early 1960s. Better known as a 'Noddy' bike, it was famed for being very quiet, an advantage when patrolling the back streets of the city.

fall foul of the changes: having answered an emergency call to a heart attack victim at a West End hotel he returned to find his Ford Popular ticketed. There was such a public outcry at his case that he was let off the £2 fine. Whether any of the other 343 recipients of tickets on that day escaped payment remains a mystery. Equally unpopular were parking meters, already on some London streets from 10 July 1958. There were those, like Councillor Stuart Edwards in Croydon – where 1,200 meters were to be installed in late 1960 – who believed that '…many people will be almost driven to leave the town.' Bristol was the first city outside of London to have meters installed, along with twenty-five traffic wardens. There were one and a half million cars registered in London by the mid-1960s, precipitating proposals for inner city parking restrictions. Belgravia residents rebelled in January 1966 when Westminster City Council put forward a scheme to introduce nearly 2,000 ten-hour meters, some of which were to be designated for residents only at a charge of 5s per day. Even though, as *The Times* reported on 20 January, the council had yet to decide 'what will constitute a resident,' local people like P. Hammond, in a letter to the editor a week later, accused the council of effectively fining them for 'parking their vehicles outside their own front

A traffic jam in
Knightsbridge,
London, mid-
1960s.

Front cover and price list from a 1965 Vespa brochure.

## PRICE LIST

as from 14th September, 1965

All the prices quoted in this list are the delivered prices recommended as appropriate for the resale of these goods.

**VESPA 90 cc.** ... ... ... ... £126 6s. 0d.
Basic Price £104 19s. 4d. Purchase Tax £21 6s. 8d.
Dual Seat, Stop Light, Steering Column Lock and Shield Protectors
Colour Finish: Fiesta Blue or Roma Red.

**VESPA 90 cc. S.S.** ... ... ... £138 14s. 3d.
Basic Price £115 5s. 8d. Purchase Tax £23 8s. 7d.
Dual Seat, Luggage and Tool Kit Compartment (with tyre and tube), Steering Column Lock and Shield Protectors Colour Finish: Roma Red or Peacock Blue

**VESPA 150 cc. G.L.** ... ... ... £177 13s. 4d.
Basic Price £148 7s. 10d. Purchase Tax £29 5s. 6d.
Dual Seat, Parking Lights, Stop Light, Steering Column Lock, Tool Box Lock and Shield Protectors. Colour Finish: Vespa Ivory or Ocean Blue

**VESPA 150 cc. SPRINT** ... ... £185 6s. 7d.
Basic Price £154 16s. 2d. Purchase Tax £30 10s. 5d.
Dual Seat, Parking Lights, Stop Light, Steering Column Lock, Tool Box Lock, Shield Protectors and Chrome Embellishments. Colour Finish: Quicksilver.

**VESPA 180 cc. S.S.** ... ... ... £214 9s. 6d.
Basic Price £179 3s. 5d. Purchase Tax £35 6s. 1d.
Dual Seat, Parking Light, Stop Light, Steering Column Lock, Spare Wheel (with tyre and tube), Shield Protectors and Luggage Compartment with Lock Colour Finish: Hawthorne White or Roma Red

A tool kit and an Operation and Maintenance Manual are supplied with each Machine

All Models Guaranteed for 6 months.

Easy Hire Purchase terms are available from all Vespa Dealers.

Always insist on Genuine Vespa Spares and Accessories.

The Company reserves the right to alter prices and specifications without prior notice

DOUGLAS (SALES & SERVICE) LTD.
KINGSWOOD, BRISTOL Tel: Bristol 67-1881/9
Division of the Westinghouse Brake and Signal Company Limited

L B 5183/30M 9 65

R.P.M (CHELMSFORD) LTD.

Telephone: 2269

**MAIN AGENTS for**

Ariel . Greeves . Honda . James
Jawa . Lambretta . Mobylette
Vespa . Velocette . Triumph . Tina

Buy your machines from the people who can give you **SERVICE** by **FACTORY TRAINED MECHANICS**

**Lambretta**

**RELIANT** DISTRIBUTORS and Service Agents

★ ★ ★

**The NEW RELIANT REGAL 3/25**

1. Powerful sealed beam headlamp and combined side light and flasher.
2. Large glove-box, windscreen demisting, air control flap for car heater, when fitted.
3. Large pockets in both doors, winding windows.
4. Spacious luggage boot with spare wheel compartment.
5. Opening quarter light for improved ventilation.
6. Rear light cluster, flashing indicator, stop light and reflector.
7. Hooded instrument panel prevents windscreen glare at night.

**26/28 BADDOW ROAD CHELMSFORD**

doors'. As more cars took to the roads, so further legislation was introduced to curb and control their drivers. Barbara Castle, the non-driving minister of transport from 1965 to 1968, imposed a 70mph speed limit on Britain's roads in January 1967, and in October that year introduced the first breathalyser tests for suspected drunken drivers.

The impact of Mods and Rockers on the 1960s transport scene was huge, for the rival gangs favoured entirely different two-wheel vehicles. The Mods in their bright, outlandish clothes, and the ubiquitous parka with the fishtail back and fur around the hood, drove around on Italian-designed Piaggio Vespas or Innocenti Lambrettas often customised with lots of mirrors on the front, which, according to John Gray from Edinburgh, were frequently stolen from cars. The Rockers went for the more aggressive motorcycles, like the Triumph Bonneville or Norton 650.

Competing gangs of Mods and Rockers often clashed, most famously along the beaches of the south coast of England over the Whitsun bank holiday, 1964. The worst violence occurred at Brighton and Margate, terrorising local residents and outraging much of the nation. Meeting up was a big part of bike culture and in Dover, members of Dover Saints Scooter Club spent many an evening with fellow scooterists outside Elizabeth's Coffee Shop in the Market Square. Rockers' favourite meeting places were cafes, including the Pelosis Italian Coffee bar near the sea front in Dover, but nowhere quite matched up to the Ace cafe on London's North Circular Road, which became a mecca for bikers.

The everyday mode of travel was bus, underground or train, or on the remaining few tram and trolley bus routes. London Transport completed their trolley bus to diesel conversion in May 1962, and introduced the double-decker Routemaster bus, with an 'open' back and grab pole and bus conductor with a ticket machine and leather bag for change. A young traveller on the Route 93 between Epsom and Putney Bridge stations was impressed by the 'comfortable brown cloth-covered seats, wind-down windows, and a long bell cord running along the nearside of their lower-deck ceiling for passengers to request the bus to stop.' London Underground's Metropolitan line, immortalised by Sir John Betjeman, was revolutionised with the introduction of roomy and light aluminium 'tube trains' in 1960, officially called A60 stock. Eleven-year-old John Farrow witnessed the first new train emerging at Moorgate, describing it as 'nothing short of a dazzling apparition' and was late for school as he took a ride to Liverpool Street and back. But it was Dr Beeching's report in March 1963 that heralded far-reaching changes to the rail network. To mitigate British Rail's huge losses, calculated at £140 million a year, over 4,000 route miles were cut on cost and efficiency grounds, and over 2,000 stations, many of them picturesque branch line halts, closed.

Competitors at the Peel Hill Climb, Isle of Man 1969.

A trolley bus near Cardiff station, 10 June 1964. Trams continued operating in the city until January 1970, while Bradford and Bournemouth were still running trolley buses until 1972. Glasgow ran its last tram on Paton Street in 1963, and was superseded by suburban railways, the underground and the diesel bus.

# RELAXATION AND ENTERTAINMENT

L ISTENING TO THE RADIO was a well-established pastime in 1960, with the BBC Light, Third and Home services offering a variety of programmes. But the appointment of Sir Hugh Greene as Director-General in January 1960 heralded great changes as programme makers were encouraged to produce material that reflected the social changes of the decade. There were any number of 'firsts' from serious news and current affairs including the *Ten o'Clock News* (1961), *The World at One* (1965) and *The World This Weekend* (1967) to comedy in the form of *Round the Horne* (1965–68), the long-running *I'm Sorry, I'll Read That Again* (1965), which originated from the Cambridge Footlights revue, *Cambridge Circus*, and the enduring *Just a Minute* (1967). Radio 1, advertised as 'the swinging new radio service' was launched by Tony Blackburn in 1967, taking *Top of the Pops* with it from the Light service, which, with the other existing channels, were renamed Radio 2, 3 and 4.

Radio undoubtedly suffered as television grew in popularity and by 1971, 91 per cent of families had a TV set, 16 per cent more than a decade earlier. Buying a set outright was costly, with a standard size 17-inch black and white model costing between 57 and 70 guineas. The greatest innovation of the decade was the introduction of colour TV in 1967, and David Wills wasted no time in buying a set, paying over £300 for his Mitsubishi model. On top of that was the increased joint licence fee of £10, introduced in January 1968. By 1972 there were more than one and a half million colour sets in use.

Around 20 million people tuned in on 10 million television sets to see the marriage of Princess Margaret to Anthony Armstrong-Jones in May 1960, the first royal wedding ever to be televised live. Soap operas like *Coronation Street*, launched tentatively by ITV in 1960, had over 20 million viewers by October 1961. The BBC's contribution, created in 1962, was the police series *Z Cars*, which addressed issues like domestic violence and teenage delinquency,

Opposite:
The police trying to keep back the crowds of hysterical fans before the northern premiere of the Beatles' film, *A Hard Day's Night*, in Liverpool, 10 July 1964.

69

National Savings Stamps were a popular savings scheme aimed at children in the 1950s and 1960s. The stamps, which featured both Prince Charles and Princess Anne, could be used to pay for a sound-only or combined TV and wireless licence. In August 1965 the combined fee rose from just over £4 to £5, while the radio-only fee went up by 50 per cent to £1 5s.

If you are a member of a National Savings stamp scheme in your street, village or place of work, you may buy stamps from your group secretary.

If you do not need to renew your licence when it expires, the stamps on the card may be used to make a deposit in the Post Office Savings Bank, Trustee Savings Bank or to buy National Savings Certificates, Development Bonds or Premium Savings Bonds. In case of need, you may obtain repayment of the value of the stamps by presenting this book at a Post Office or Trustee Savings Bank.

IF FOUND PLEASE RETURN THIS CARD TO:

MR. MRS. MISS._____

ADDRESS_____

51.2921 J.B.Ltd.

**WIRELESS LICENCE**

**Savings Card**

## Why not save for your next licence

This card will help you to do so. Whenever you can, buy a 2/6 National Savings stamp and stick it on this card. Then when you are taking out your next licence, hand in this card and the value of all the stamps on it will count towards the cost.

FOR A SOUND ONLY LICENCE YOU NEED TEN 2/6 STAMPS (£1. 5s. 0d.)

FOR A COMBINED SOUND AND TELEVISION LICENCE YOU NEED FORTY 2/6 STAMPS (£5)

| 25 | 26 | 27 | 28 |
|----|----|----|----|
| £2. 0. 0. to save | £1. 17. 6. to save | £1. 15. 0. to save | £1. 12. 6. to save |
| 29 | 30 | 31 | 32 |
| £1. 10. 0. to save | £1. 7. 6. to save | £1. 5. 0. to save | £1. 2. 6. to save |
| 33 | 34 | 35 | 36 |
| £1. 0. 0. to save | 17/6 to save | 15/- to save | 12/6 to save |
| 37 | 38 | 39 | 40 |
| 10/- to save | 7/6 to save | 5/- to save | 2/6 to save |

FOR A SOUND ONLY LICENCE £1. 5. 0. START AT SQUARE 31

ONLY 2/6 NATIONAL SAVINGS STAMPS SHOULD BE USED ON THIS CARD.

YOU CAN BUY NATIONAL SAVINGS STAMPS AT MOST POST OFFICES, SOME TRUSTEE SAVINGS BANKS, AND FROM NATIONAL SAVING GROUPS AND CENTRES.

| 9 | 10 | 11 | 12 |
|----|----|----|----|
| £4. 0. 0. to save | £3. 17. 6. to save | £3. 15. 0. to save | £3. 12. 6. to save |
| 13 | 14 | 15 | 16 |
| £3. 10. 0. to save | £3. 7. 6. to save | £3. 5. 0. to save | £3. 2. 6. to save |
| 3 | 4 | 17 | 18 | 19 | 20 |
| £4. 15. 0. to save | £4. 12. 6. to save | £3. 0. 0. to save | £2. 17. 6. to save | £2. 15. 0. to save | £2. 12. 6. to save |
| 5 | 6 | 7 | 8 | 21 | 22 | 23 | 24 |
| £4. 10. 0. to save | £4. 7. 6. to save | £4. 5. 0. to save | £4. 2. 6. to save | £2. 10. 0. to save | £2. 7. 6. to save | £2. 5. 0. to save | £2. 2. 6. to save |

FOR A COMBINED SOUND AND TELEVISION LICENCE COMPLETE 40 SPACES

The alternative to purchasing a TV outright was to buy on hire purchase or rent from companies like Radio Rentals or DER (Domestic Electric Rentals), which meant an outlay of around 9s 6d a week, inclusive of free maintenance, insurance and an aerial.

and controversially portrayed police officers with their own marriage problems, gambling habits and bullying tendencies. This incensed the Chief Constable of Lancashire, Sir Eric St Johnston, who failed to stop the programme being aired. The numbers of viewers of *Z Cars* peaked at 17 million in 1963. Other innovative programmes included *Dr Finlay's Casebook* and an entirely new sitcom, *Steptoe and Son*, with its cunning, unsuccessful rag and bone man and ambitious son airing their opposing political views. The influence of the Cold War was evident in series like *Danger Man* in 1960 and *The Saint*, broadcast from 1966 to 1969, but it was *The Avengers*, first piloted in January 1961, with Steed and Mrs Emma Peel, and *The Prisoner*, created by and starring Patrick McGoohan, which ran from September 1967 to February 1968, that acquired cult status. Science fiction was served well by *Dr Who*, which ran initially from 1963 to 1989. Serious drama was not neglected, and the BBC's Wednesday Play, introduced in 1964, gained a reputation for tackling contemporary social issues, the most outstanding being *Up the Junction* in November 1965 and *Cathy Come Home* in November 1966. The commercial channel, ITV, was in its infancy but was proving to be, as predicted, 'a licence to print money.' In the ten years from 1960 annual advertising expenditure rose from

£76 Million to £93 Million with the company making an annual profit of 130 per cent. One Birmingham teenager thought the adverts were as entertaining as the programmes, with jingles for Omo, Pepsodent, Esso and Clinic shampoo staying firmly lodged in his mind. ITV's children's series, *Thunderbirds*, launched in 1965 and enjoyed enormous success, as did the BBC's *Play School* (1964) and *The Magic Roundabout* (1965). The popularity of *Blue Peter*, originally launched in 1958, was evident as the programme began airing twice a week rather than once from 1960.

Satire hit BBC television in 1962, with *That Was The Week That Was*, informally known as *TW3*, and hosted by twenty-two-year-old David Frost. Every week Millicent Martin belted out the theme tune, with words reflecting the week's news. Frost and his ruthlessly funny young team, which included Roy Kinnear, Willie Rushton and Lance Percival, then proceeded to heap scorn on world events and the government. Audiences first experienced *Monty Python's Flying Circus* – with its silly songs, 'Spam' sketch and dead parrots – in October 1969, by which time the British population were familiar with the campaigning voice of Mrs

Mary Whitehouse, the self-appointed guardian of Britain's moral standards. Her first public meeting in April 1964 was attended by over 2,000 people and in 1965, through her National Viewers' and Listeners' Association, she amassed a record 500,000 signatures for her 'Clean-Up TV' petition, which was even sent to the Queen.

The 1962 Pilkington Committee's report on the future of broadcasting resulted in the launch of BBC2, the third national channel, in April 1964, although all the audience got the first night was Gerald Priestland apologising for a blackout, caused by a power failure at the Alexandra Palace studio. The new channel was renowned for producing landmark documentaries including *The Great War* in 1964 and *Civilisation* in 1967. By then, programmes were being beamed by satellite across the world via Telstar, revolutionising popular entertainment and bringing American programmes into British homes.

Nothing came to define the 1960s as much as popular music. In January 1963, Elvis Presley, Cliff Richard – who went on to have more chart hits than the Beatles and Rolling Stones combined – Frank Ifield, and the Shadows were among the top names in the *New Musical Express* charts and by 1961, the BBC's panel programme, *Juke Box Jury*, had more than 12 million viewers. Associated Rediffusion's programme *Ready, Steady Go*, launched in August 1963, was as much about the music as it was about circulating the latest trends and fashions to teenage audiences the length and breadth of the country. Among the female vocalists to acquire celebrity status were Dusty Springfield, Lulu, Helen Shapiro and Sandie Shaw, who was the first person to win the Eurovision Song Contest for the UK in 1967. But it was the Beatles, a group of four would-be rock and roll musicians from Liverpool, who became the phenomenon of the decade. Their October 1962 debut single,

Sales figures for 7-inch 45rpm vinyl records grew from four million in 1955, to 52 million in 1960, and to 61 million just three years later. Teenagers made up almost half of the market for records and record players.

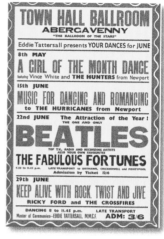

Posters for Beatles appearances, New Brighton, Liverpool 1961 and Abergavenny, June 1963, and a ticket from a gig where the Rolling Stones appeared, October 1963.

'Love Me Do', peaked at seventeenth in the chart and 'Please Please Me' made it to number one in March 1963, followed by 'From Me to You' released a month later. Liverpool and the Cavern, where the Beatles played, became a new landmark and Beatlemania swept the country. When fifteen-year-old Diane L heard the group were going to play in her local town in Yorkshire in November 1963, albeit as a supporting act to the chart-topping Helen Shapiro, she and her friend determined to get tickets. Unbeknown to her parents, they crept out of the house in the dead of night and walked into town to join the queue. Although they didn't get front-row seats they 'got a good view of the Fab Four. As to hearing anything they actually sang – well, no – but that was not the point!' The Beatles' fame and fortune gathered momentum, with success after success, including the award of MBEs by the Queen in 1965. The group played together for the last time on 30 January 1969, with their final album, *Abbey Road*, released the following September to universal acclaim. Meanwhile the popularity of the Rolling Stones was growing, even though they were described by the *Daily Express* in 1964 as 'five tough young London-based music makers with doorstep mouths, pallid cheeks and unkempt hair.' The Beatles and the Rolling Stones featured regularly on Radio Caroline, the most notable of the pirate radio stations. Launched in international waters on Easter Sunday 1964, the station played pop music all day and attracted tens of millions of listeners, making disc jockeys like Tony Blackburn, Simon Dee and Roger Day household names overnight.

Reading remained hugely popular, with borrowing from libraries increasing hugely during the decade. Local authorities doubled their spending following the introduction, in 1965, of the Public Libraries and Museums Act, 1964. Basic lending and reference services were free, and more than 600 million books were issued by 1970, an increase of 203 million on 1959. Casualties were private subscription libraries including W. H. Smith & Son, who closed their remaining 286 circulation library branches on 27 May 1961, and Boots Booklovers' Library, whose last branch closed in 1966. New technology impacted on sales, with Penguin the leading producers of affordable paperback books. Eye-catching modern covers revitalised their image and they increased the number of titles from around 6,000 in 1960 to 37,000 by the end of the decade. Penguin's

Folk singers entertaining the crowds on Portobello Road, Notting Hill, London on a Saturday afternoon in 1966.

publication of *Lady Chatterley's Lover*, the subsequent trial in 1960 under the Obscene Publications Act 1959, and the publisher's acquittal not only marked a turning point in British censorship laws, but was a boost to sales, which reached two million copies in just six weeks. One Durham university student bought his mother a copy who, having read it, pronounced it to be 'just like real life.' Male readers favoured Ian Fleming's stories of James Bond, John le Carré's spy thrillers and Alastair MacLean's titles, eighteen of which, including *Where Eagles Dare*, sold more than one million copies. Women readers preferred authors like Georgette Heyer, Barbara Cartland and Agatha Christie, as well as anything published by Mills & Boon. Readers of *The Sunday Times* were the first in the world to have a full-colour magazine supplement in February 1962, which included the first ever full-page colour advertisement. *The Sun* newspaper was launched in August 1964, but despite a huge initial readership, it quickly declined and by mid-1969 was sold by owners IPC to Rupert Murdoch.

On stage, *Beyond the Fringe*, which opened at the tiny Fortune Theatre in London on 10 May 1961, was the touchpaper for the satire boom of the 1960s. A professional comedy revue, the cardigan-clad team of Dudley Moore, Jonathan Miller, Peter Cook and Alan Bennett were applauded by the critics, especially Bernard Levin, who described it in the *Daily Express* as 'a revue so brilliant, adult, hard-boiled, accurate, merciless, witty, unexpected, alive, exhilarating, cleansing, right, true, and good that my first conscious thought as I stumbled, weak and sick with laughter, up the stairs at the end was one of gratitude'. On the back of this success, Peter Cook opened The Establishment Club in Soho, and the satirical magazine, *Private Eye*, appeared on bookstalls across Britain, with the exception of W. H. Smith, which refused to stock the 6d paper. British cinema played a key part in defining the country's new identity, and, like TV, reflected the emerging cultural and social shift of the decade in films like *Saturday Night and Sunday Morning* (1960). The James Bond films, starting with *Dr No* in 1963, carried an anti-communist message which may not have been taken very seriously. And even though the films were hugely successful, their popularity was not enough to stop the decline in cinema attendance, which dropped from around 500 million in 1960 to 193 million by 1970.

Betting shops opened at a rate of 100 a week, with about 10,000 set up between May and November 1961, while about 1,000

The Rolling Stones were amongst the scheduled guests on *Ready, Steady, Go*, aired on 26 June 1964. Left to right: Bill Wyman (guitar); Brian Jones (guitar); Charlie Watts (drum); Mick Jagger (vocal); Keith Richards (guitar).

The Essoldo, Caledonian Road, London, c. 1967. The Essoldo was one of many cinemas converted to a bingo hall once the game was legalised by the new Betting and Gaming Act 1960.

Opposite: World champion angler, Billy Lanes, on a riverbank, surrounded by maggots, 8 December 1963. Fishing was the most popular participatory sport during the 1960s, and by 1970 there were 3.5 million regular anglers.

casinos were opened in the first five years following the introduction of the Betting and Gaming Act in 1960. Of all the sports enjoyed in the 1960s, which ranged from badminton to speedway and horse racing, county cricket was considered to be the national team sport, but by the mid-1960s association football in England, and rugby union in Wales, had overtaken it in popularity. This was partly due to television, which proved to be the perfect medium for transmitting a ninety-minute match to folk in the comfort of their living rooms. When the World Cup was played between England and West Germany at Wembley on 30 July 1966, 32 million people tuned in and saw twenty-five-year-old Bobby Moore's team win the cup for the first time in British history. Spectators like Alan Haycock paid £3 10s for their ten-match World Cup ticket, which he considered to be 'the best value ever'. For their success, members of the English team were each paid a bonus of £1,000. By then, the official maximum weekly wage for footballers of £20 had been abolished, and in 1962 England midfielder, Johnny Haynes, at Fulham, became the first player to receive £100 a week, rather less than George Best's weekly earnings of £5,000 in 1969.

# WORK

THE POPULAR VIEW of the early 1960s is of a buoyant economy, high levels of employment, low inflation and rising wages – the average weekly earnings for a man over twenty-one were £15 35s in 1961 and had risen to £23 by 1968. Combined, these fuelled a general improvement in living standards and the growth of a consumer society.

But there was another 'England' with areas of high unemployment and deprivation, especially in the north and north-east of the country. Even educated girls with a General Certificate of Education could only aspire to working as a shop assistant, and many young people went straight from school via the employment exchange to the dole queue. Between 1960 and 1962 some 3,000 people migrated south from the north-east, with another 10,000 following in 1963, all seeking work. When, in 1964, the national average for unemployment was 1.9 per cent, the rate in Falmouth had reached 10.8 per cent, a tenth of the community's workers. Traditional industries, like mining and fisheries in Cornwall, were rapidly disappearing, and cotton mills in Lancashire were closing at the rate of one a week in the 1960s and 1970s. The riverside industry was also in decline, and work, which was never permanent, became harder to obtain. The men moved from wharf to wharf depending on how many were needed for a shipment, and it was up to the dock master to choose employees, causing a lot of competitiveness between workers. Pay was dependent on the tonnage moved.

By the early 1960s four out of ten married women in their forties and fifties, whose children were off their hands, were in paid work, but one in three husbands interviewed in 1965 were still unhappy about their womenfolk having jobs. There were also two million working women with school-age children. An expanding group with younger children could not rely upon any state help with childcare, for the prevailing view, largely driven by economics, was that it was up to them to reconcile work and family responsibilities. Wherever they

Opposite: Women operating early mainframe computers for HSBC in 1962. In the 1960s women under twenty-four years old were paid the same as men, but above that age salaries differed, except for women who were in the proficiency grade. By 1963 the bank were allowing married women a reasonable period of maternity leave, but without pay and without credit for pension purposes.

A Career with Woolworth

In the 1960s a typical Woolworth's sales assistant was paid £6 for a forty-hour, four-and-a-half-day week, which included three Saturdays in four. Fifteen-year-old juniors and Saturday staff – mostly school children as young as thirteen – were paid 7d per hour. Stores normally had an early closing day, giving staff an afternoon off mid-week.

worked, women were paid less than their male counterparts, had fewer opportunities and were generally considered to be unreliable, inferior and weak. Even though the job choice for fifteen-year-old girl school leavers in the early 1960s was limited, Jo Chisholm celebrated the end of restrictions, rules and regulations which were replaced by the freedom to wear what she liked, go where she wanted and to enjoy '…freedom, love, flowers and bells!' F. W. Woolworth was typical in employing girls and women in junior roles and the men as managers and executives, but Sainsbury's had a more enlightened approach, as one school leaver interviewed for an episode of the BBC schools television programme, *Going to Work*, first broadcast in the 1960s, revealed. Not only did the company pay £1 5s more than the minimum weekly rate for shop work of £3 5s but they believed in promoting from the shop floor. Maureen was impressed that 'many of the top people in the company started at the bottom' and valued the fact that she got 'a full day off every week to go to technical college' and that her fares and fees were paid for. Most of the girls Pauline Mounsey knew went into office jobs, but the GPO turned her down as she failed the spelling test. Girls employed as secretaries, either in an office or a huge typing pool, took notes and memos in shorthand and then typed them up on manual typewriters. Ruth's first job was for Reid and Welsh Ltd, Lossiebank Mills based in Elgin, which paid better money than Woolworth's. Pay at the mill, where all the weavers were women and were paid less than the male warpers, was on a piece rate so hard work was well rewarded, but staff who arrived even a few minutes after 8 a.m. had their pay docked. Working the looms was rough, dirty, noisy and involved some heavy lifting, and there was little or no safety protection from shuttles that flew out, injuring staff. Fifteen-year-old Roy Downton had no trouble finding a job, and took up an apprenticeship, for which he was paid £2 10s a week. Apart from giving his mother £1 10s for his keep, the rest was his to spend as he liked, as there was no income tax to pay until the age of eighteen.

The immigrant work experience was very different, for discrimination was rife and many highly qualified incomers had to settle for menial jobs. There were well-educated teachers from Nairobi working at the Post Office, barristers from Pakistan doing labouring jobs, and a customs inspector earning a wage as a railway cleaner. The first, and controversial, Commonwealth Immigrants Bill became law on 1 July 1962, and introduced a quota system that limited the numbers of migrants into Britain from Commonwealth countries, including India and east and west Pakistan. The initial response to the act was a tremendous drop in the number of incomers, as the promise of the bill had sparked a rush of people into Britain before the doors were closed. The industrial centres of the Midlands and north of England became home to many men like Boshir, who arrived in 1963. As an unskilled worker he initially joined a cotton mill in Darlington, before quickly moving to 'a better job in the sugar mills in Preston, Lancashire...the best mill in England' where he worked shifts. Essential staff, including doctors and nurses, were needed to address the shortages in the rapidly expanding NHS, and were

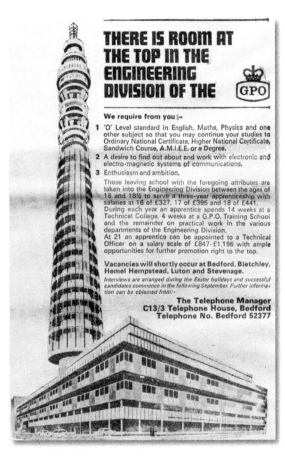

An advertisement from the *Bletchley District Gazette*, 1967, for apprenticeships with the GPO, features the iconic Post Office Tower in the background.

excluded from the quota. Existing official nursing recruitment programmes in the Caribbean continued and by the end of 1965, there were between 3,000 and 5,000 Jamaican nurses working in British hospitals, many of them concentrated in London and the Midlands. Esme found it very hard working as an auxiliary nurse, having left her two children behind in Jamaica, and she sent most of her £5 weekly wage home to pay for their upkeep. By 1960 between 30 and 40 per cent of all junior doctors in the NHS were from India, Pakistan, Bangladesh and Sri Lanka. This first wave was followed in 1963 by a further 18,000 or so trained doctors from overseas, including India and Pakistan, who were recruited as a result of a campaign initiated by Enoch Powell, but by 1968 he was less happy about immigrants.

There were just over nine million trade union members in 1962, a figure that had risen to more than ten million by the late 1960s. While

A meeting during the seamen's strike, held at the Mill Dam South Shields, Jim Slater of the National Union of Seamen is seated behind the microphone on 1 January 1960.

the election-campaigning Conservative government boasted in 1964 that they were responsible for keeping strike rates lower than any Western country, bar Germany, unofficial wildcat strikes were disrupting business and the economy, and had earned the unions, and the shop stewards, a reputation for what Dominic Sandbrook called their 'militant unruliness.' There were fewer than three million working days lost each year to strikes – wildcat and official – from 1962, but as industrial unrest began to surface, this figure reached 4.7 million days in 1968. Among the strikers were 160,000 Post Office workers who were refused a 4 per cent wage rise, and spent a month on work-to-rule in early 1961. A walk out by twenty-two staff at Girling's brake factory in Cheshire, already the victim of fifty-seven separate disputes in eighteen months, brought the car industry to a halt with 5,000 workers laid off at other plants. But the worst was the official strike called in February 1969 at the Ford Motor Company, which virtually halted production and seriously affected exports. As unofficial 'wild-cat' strikes became more frequent, and the trade unions began to flex their muscles, the general public quickly lost sympathy. Relations between Harold Wilson, George Brown and the unions was at rock bottom and when thousands of dockers went on strike in September 1967, the ports of Liverpool, Manchester, Hull and London were immobilised and the trade deficit more than doubled to £107 million by October.

Later in the decade the women's liberation movement made slow inroads against the old barriers and inequalities. When 187 female car-seat cover machinists at the Ford car plant in Dagenham, Essex, walked out on strike in 1968, they not only brought car production to a halt, with the lay-off of thousands of workers, but they struck a blow for unequal pay and paved the way for the 1970 Equal Pay Act. In 1969, a propaganda film made by the Central Office of Information for Department of Employment appeared to be addressing teenage girls, who were 'leaving school without thinking about further education or training'. The implied message was 'don't be tempted by the short-term rewards of unskilled jobs, because a career will serve you better in the long run.' It had a 1960s soundtrack and animation style, and the girl was wearing knee-length boots, micro-dress and headband. 'However, in the voice over a middle-aged man addressed the parents rather than girls themselves, suggesting that some parents also needed convincing of the value of long-term goals for their daughters'. By the late 1960s more than two million women and eight million men in jobs – ranging from bus conductors to ballet dancers – belonged to a trade union.

Three female bus conductresses campaigning for equal pay and rights with men at a demonstration in London's Trafalgar Square, 1968.

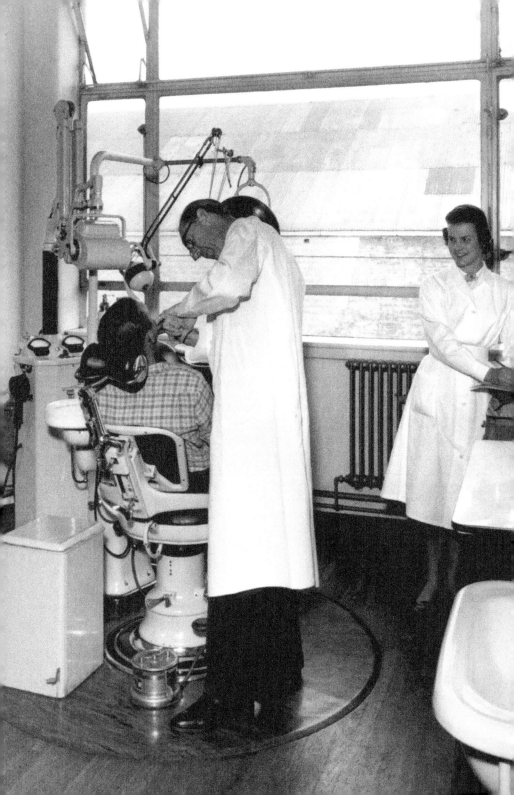

# HEALTH

A COMBINATION of scientific discoveries and the benefits of the
National Health Service had a huge impact on the health of the
nation in the 1960s. Hearing aids were inspired by the development
of the transistor radio, and innovative behind-the-ear and spectacle
aids replaced the bulky ones worn across the body. Advances in x-ray
equipment owed much to research in the photographic industry, and
chemical engineering impacted on the production of new drugs.
Among these was the broad-spectrum penicillin, ampicillin, which
was introduced by Beecham in 1961, and was used extensively to treat
bacterial infections. Levodopa was found to help Parkinson's disease
sufferers, making this the first time a biochemical mechanism had
been found to treat the symptoms of a neurological disease. Sufferers
of rheumatism, arthritis and gout were offered effective pain relief by
the new drug indomethacin, released in 1965. The latest
antidepressant drugs enabled many mentally ill patients to be treated
without admission to hospital. The 1964 Drugs (Prevention of Misuse)
Act made the possession of un-prescribed amphetamines – the Purple
Hearts, Black Bombers and French Blues taken by partying youngsters
– an offence, but from 1966 cannabis, which sold on the streets for
about £7 an ounce, and to a lesser extent, LSD, became the fashionable
recreational drugs. They too were prohibited by a succession of Drugs
Acts in the 1960s.

In ophthalmology, newly developed lasers were used to treat
detached retinas and vascular abnormalities. Asthma sufferers
welcomed the new pressurised inhalers from 1959 but the 'epidemic'
of asthma deaths from unknown causes resulted in a warning in 1967
about the possible danger of these aerosols. The Sabin polio vaccine,
easily administered orally on a sugar lump, replaced Salk in 1962, and
was included in the routine vaccination programme. The introduction
of a measles vaccine in the UK in 1968 had an almost immediate
impact on the number of notified cases, which dropped from around

Opposite:
Among the welfare
provisions made
for workers at the
Pressed Steel
Company car body
plant in Cowley,
Oxfordshire, was a
fully equipped
dental surgery.
They also had a
doctor and a
physiotherapist.
The company
employed 22,170
people in 1961.

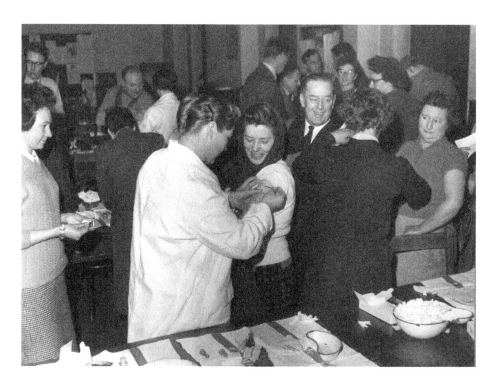

Doctors in Manchester town hall vaccinating members of the public against smallpox, during a health scare, on 15 January 1962. Despite the Ministry of Health assurance that the outbreak was under control, queues formed outside doctors' surgeries and some three million people were vaccinated.

450,000 cases a year to 300,000 by 1970, with deaths down from 100 to around fifty per year.

The decade was marked by milestones in surgery that changed people's lives. The first living donor kidney transplant was performed by Sir Michael Woodruff at Edinburgh Royal Infirmary in 1960 and involved a set of identical forty-nine-year-old twins. The medical superintendent was right when he remarked 'I think the recipient has a sporting chance of getting away with it', for the patient went back to work after fifteen weeks and lived for a further six years, as did his twin, before dying of cancer. Professor John Charnley, who had devoted years to research and development, carried out the first full hip replacement in November 1962, and in May 1968, South African surgeon Donald Ross carried out Britain's first heart transplant at the National Heart Hospital in Marylebone, London.

For all these advancements, the 1960s were blighted by the tragedy of the drug thalidomide, marketed as Distaval, which was prescribed to women in early pregnancy to treat morning sickness. There were some 466 babies born in Britain between 1958 and 1961 with a variety of limb deformities and some also had damage to their internal organs. In 1968 the UK manufacturer Distillers Biochemicals Ltd reached a financial settlement after a legal battle with the families of those affected, but the fight for a realistic compensation package continued long after the 1960s. The thalidomide disaster and evidence of the unsuspected side effects of certain medicines led to the formation of the Dunlop Committee on the Safety of Drugs in 1963, which devised a system of checking new drugs from January 1964. The yellow card system followed so that rare reactions could be notified.

Cancer was, as ever, a scourge, with the number of deaths exceeding 100,000 for the first time ever in 1962. Diagnosis and treatment was left to surgeons and radiotherapists as there were very few medical oncologists. In the late 1960s fewer than three children in ten survived their disease for at least five years. Dying and terminally ill adults found a champion in Cicely Saunders, who founded St Christopher's Hospice in south London in 1967. Saunders, who was made a Dame in 1979, changed end-of-life care, pioneering holistic care in purpose-built surroundings.

For women the introduction of cervical screening in 1966 was a step in the right direction, but there was no comprehensive programme set up, many high-risk women slipped through the net, and the follow-up procedures for those who had been tested positive were inefficient. In theory, the oral contraceptive, first marketed in Britain in 1963, was to set women free from unwanted pregnancy but in practice the government made it very difficult for unmarried women to obtain the pill, as they did not want to be seen to be encouraging pre-marital sex, or 'free love', and it was 1964 before doctors could prescribe it for single women. The Family Planning Association began providing contraceptive advice to single women in 1966, and although the Family Planning Act, 1967, allowed local authorities to provide free family planning services, only about one quarter did so. The cost to the NHS was just over 1s a pill – and some politicians worried that it would be a huge financial burden on the Treasury. By the end of the 1960s only one woman in ten had ever taken the pill.

Few smokers paid attention to the risk of lung cancer before the Royal College of Physicians launched their report, *Smoking and Health* in 1962. The warning was unequivocal and instigated the banning of cigarette advertising on television in 1965.

Up until 1967, abortion was technically illegal, and women's groups and the pro-abortion lobby continued their campaign, with several unsuccessful bills in 1953, 1961, 1965 and 1966. Joan G had an abortion in 1960 and recounted her experience:

> two Harley St psychiatrists, a doctor in a seedy surgery in Half Moon Street then the abortion in Ealing. Parents in 1960 were not willing to discuss such 'disgusting happenings'. I was on my own, you were made to feel dirty by the doctors etc, my father would not speak to me for 5–6 months, and I was forever made to feel unclean.

The 1967 Abortion Act legalised abortion during the first twenty-eight weeks of pregnancy for all women, not only when the life of the mother was in danger as was previously the law, and in the first eleven months eight doctors each carried out more than 500 abortions.

The state of the nation's teeth was a huge concern throughout the decade with the incidence of dental disease and decay higher than ever. While examinations, the arrest of bleeding and domiciliary visits remained free, charges had been introduced – except for those under twenty-one, and expectant and recently delivered mothers – and increased in the 1960s. In May 1961 treatment was £1, or the full cost had to be paid if less than £1. This went up to £1 5s in 1969. For dentures and bridges the maximum charge per course was £5, which increased to £6 5s in August 1969. In 1966 there were 12,000 dentists in Britain and about 11 million adults with dentures, with the basic Health Service set cost varying between £3 10s and £4 10s. By comparison a privately made set cost anything from £14 upwards, but more people were prepared to pay for these. Prescription charges were abolished in 1965 but were re-introduced in June 1968, with certain specified long-term conditions qualifying for exemption from charges.

Up until the late 1960s local health authorities issued tokens for free milk, vitamins and orange juice in its distinctive brown bottle for pre-school children. Medical care in schools was provided by the visiting school nurse, who checked for head lice and undertook routine eye and hearing tests, and by the school dental service. This was, according to the British Dental Association, near breaking point in 1960, and with only one dental officer to every 7,000–10,000 children, inspection and treatment were worse than ten years earlier. On average, most of them saw the school dentist only once in three years. In 1961, only half of the 17 million children in Local Authority (LA) schools had their teeth inspected and of the 50 per cent who needed treatment only about 17 per cent actually got it. To work properly, the service needed to double the number of dentists, but with a starting salary of £1,100, rising to a maximum of £1,735 after eight years, there was little inducement for newly qualified dentists to enter the school service. In 1969, around 90 per cent of children under twelve suffered from dental caries, and while fluoridation of the water had been shown to substantially improve the teeth of young children, it was not universally accepted. Ninety-two local authorities were hindered from introducing it as they shared water supplies with opposing authorities. With no government policy forthcoming, in 1969 a group of concerned multi-disciplinary professionals founded the British Fluoridation Society, hoping to improve uptake. New battery-operated toothbrushes helped encourage even the smallest child to clean their teeth, with Mothercare introducing one with four separate brushes in 1969 at a cost of 3 guineas.

Children in hospital still fared badly, despite the recommendations of the 1959 Platt Report, which included unlimited parental visiting. This had not been implemented at the Queen Elizabeth Hospital, Hackney Road, London in 1961, and the two weeks that young Simon Webb spent there were utter misery. After one of his mother's time-restricted visits he cried bitterly, and was warned by the Sister that if he

The busy out-patients department at Coventry and Warwickshire Hospital, Stoney Stanton Road, Coventry, on 16 November 1964.

carried on, she would not be allowed to see him at all. Improvements in care were slow, with the first hospital play group in the UK opened by Save the Children at the Brook Hospital, London in 1963. There were many more paediatricians appointed in the 1960s due to the interest in paediatric disease and realisation that lives could be saved.

During the 1960s the number of people covered by private medical insurance almost doubled from around one million to two million. Being overweight in the 1960s was unusual, with only 1–2 per cent of adults rated as obese, but 66 per cent of 1,900 people surveyed in 1967 said they wanted to lose up to a stone, and nine out of ten of them had tried to lose weight in the past year.

In an effort to address the shortage of hospitals, the government announced a ten-year hospital building programme in 1962, which approved the development of district general hospitals for population areas of about 125,000. Olivia Brittain started her nurse training in the Victoria Infirmary in Glasgow in 1963, and chose the hospital because her brother had been well-treated there after an accident and she liked the ward-based method of teaching. Nursing standards were very strict, and there was a very clear hierarchy which Angela Evans, who was state registered in London in 1963, remembered: 'Ward sister was very powerful and very visible, as was the night sister. When you were on a night shift, the night sister would come round at least twice every night, expecting a report on every patient and making sure the sluice was spotless.' And as Christine Hancock recalled, in 1966 'everything from uniform, personal behaviour and the way patients were treated was regimented at every level.' But change was on the way: the first nursing degrees were introduced in Edinburgh in 1960, followed by the launch of an investigation into nurse education by the Royal College of Nursing, under the chairmanship of Sir Henry Platt. The resulting report, *Reform of Nursing Education* (1964), which proposed two different courses – one for registered nurses and one for enrolled nurses – was accepted by the college council. It took longer for the government to deal with the shortage of general practitioners, a situation that was exacerbated by the 1957 Willink Committee, which had cut medical student numbers. Too few doctors were trying to look after too many patients, and many had far more than the permitted maximum 3,500 patients on their list. Others, like the general practitioner interviewed in a BBC2 broadcast in February 1965, was seeing between seventy-five and 100 patients a day. In 1961, Lord Cohen of Birkenhead told the House of Lords: 'The Health Service would have collapsed if it had not been for the enormous influx from junior doctors from such countries as India and Pakistan.'

Opposite:
A male district nurse helping a patient to walk, 1967.

# PLACES TO VISIT

*Ace Cafe*, London, Ace Corner, North Circular Road, London, NW10 7UD. Tel: 020 8961 1000. Website: www.ace-cafe-london.com/

*The Beatles Story Albert Dock*, Brittania Vaults, Albert Dock, Liverpool, L3 4AD. Tel: 0151 709 1963. Website: www.beatlesstory.com

*The Design Museum,* London. For location and opening hours visit the website: www.designmuseum.org

*Greater Manchester Police Museum &Archives*, 57a Newton Street, Northern Quarter, Manchester, M1 1ET. Tel: 0161 8563287/4500.

*Heritage Motor Centre*, Banbury Road, Gaydon, Warwickshire, CV35 0BJ. Tel: 01926 641188. Website: www.heritage-motor-centre.co.uk

*The Hovercraft Museum*, Daedalus Site, Argus Gate, Chark Lane, Gosport, Lee-on-the-Solent, Hampshire, PO13 9NY. Tel: 02392 525090. Website: www.hovercraft-museum.org

*Haynes International Motor Museum*, Sparkford, Yeovil, Somerset, BA22 7LH. Tel: 01963 440 804. Website: www.haynesmotormuseum.com

*London Transport Museum*, Covent Garden Piazza, London, WC2E 7BB. Tel: 020 7379 6344. Website: www.ltmuseum.co.uk

*Museum of Brands, Packaging and Advertising*, 2 Colville Mews, Lonsdale Road, Notting Hill, London, W11 2AR. Tel: 020 7908 0880. Website: www.museumofbrands.com

*National Media Museum*, Bradford, West Yorkshire, BD1 1NQ. Website: www.nationalmediamuseum.org.uk

*National Museum of British Popular Culture*, Land of Lost Content, The Market Hall, Market Street, Craven Arms, Shropshire, SY7 9NW. Tel: 01588 676176. Website: www.lolc.org.uk

*Victoria and Albert Museum*, Cromwell Road, London, SW7 2RL. Tel: 020 7942 2000. Wesbite: www.vam.ac.uk For 1960s fashion and textiles.

*West Wales Museum of Childhood*, Pen-ffynnon, Llangeler, Carmarthenshire, SA44 5EY. Tel: 01559 370428. Website: www.toymuseumwales.co.uk

*F. W. Woolworth*, for a complete history visit www.woolworthsmuseum.co.uk

*Butlin's*, for information visit www.butlinsmemories.com

*Dover Saints Scooter Club*, for information visit www.doversaintssc.co.uk

# FURTHER READING

Miriam Akhtar and Steve Humphries. *Some Liked it Hot. The British on Holiday at Home and Abroad*. Virgin, 2000.

Miriam Akhtar and Steve Humphries. *The Fifties and Sixties. A Lifestyle Revolution*. Macmillan, 2002.

Gareth Brown. *Mods and Rockers: The Origins and Era of a Modern Scene*. Independent Music Press, Shropshire, 2010.

James Chapman. *Saints and Avengers. British Adventure Series of the 1960s*. I. B. Tauris, London and New York, 2002.

Richard Davenport-Hines. *An English Affair. Sex, Class and Power in the Age of Profumo*. Harper Press, 2013.

Gerard DeGroot. *The Sixties Unplugged*. Pan Macmillan, 2013.

Mark Donnelly. *Sixties Britain, Culture, Society and Politics*. Pearson Education Ltd, Harlow, Essex, 2005.

Anna Flowers & Vanessa Histon (eds). *It's My Life. 1960s Newcastle*. Tyne Bridge Publishing, Newcastle, 2009.

Juliet Gardiner. *From the Bomb to the Beatles. The changing face of post-war Britain 1945–1965*. Collins & Brown, 1999.

Richard Holt. *Sport and the British. A Modern History*. Oxford University Press, Oxford, 1990.

Stuard Hylton. *Magical History Tour: The 1960s Revisited*. Sutton Publishing, Stroud, Gloucestershire, 2000.

Andrew Marr. *A History of Modern Britain*. Macmillan, 2007.

Arthur Marwick. *British Society since 1945*. 4th ed. Penguin, 2003.

Robert Opie. *1960s Scrapbook*. pi Global Publishing, 1999.

Danny Powell. *Studying British Cinema. The 1960s*. Auteur, Leighton Buzzard, Bedfordshire, 2009.

Alison Pressley. *The 50s and 60s. The Best of Times. Growing up and being young in Britain*. Index, 2007.

John Pressnell. *The Mini*. Shire, Oxford, 2004.

John Pressnell. *Mini – The Definitive History*. Haynes, Bristol, 2009.

Dominic Sandbrook. *Never Had it So Good. A History of Britain from Suez to the Beatles*. Abacus, 2006.

Dominic Sandbrook. *White Heat. A History of Britain in the Swinging Sixties*. Abacus, 2007.

Pat Thane & Tanya Evans. 'The Permissive Society. Unmarried Mothers in the 1960s', in *Sinners? Scroungers? Saints? Unmarried Motherhood in Twentieth-Century England*. Oxford University Press, 2012.

Ben Thompson. *Ban This Filth. Letters From the Mary Whitehouse Archive*. Faber and Faber, 2012.

Richard Weight. *Mod: A Very British Style*. The Bodley Head, 2013.

# INDEX